KILLING WITH IMPUNITY

WRITHING SILHOUETTES

I0165053

BY
ROBERT ALGERI
Author of Suspenseful Fiction and Crime Thrillers

PUBLICATION CONSULTANTS
WE BELIEVE IN THE POWER OF AUTHORS

PO Box 221974 Anchorage, Alaska 99522-1974
books@publicationconsultants.com—www.
publicationconsultants.com

DISCLAIMER

Following is a work of fiction based on actual events.

Any resemblance to actual persons, living or dead, is purely coincidental and unintentional. The people and places are products of the author's imagination.

Events surrounding the case of prolific Alaskan serial killer Robert Hansen provide the backdrop for this story. In 1983, Robert Hansen admitted to killing seventeen women. Police suspect he may have killed many more. Robert Hansen died in 2014. As of January 4, 2020, eleven of the victims have been found and recovered; six of the women are still missing.

Law Enforcement has been puzzled by the lack of information regarding the remaining victims. In mid-April 2020, Alaska State Trooper Cold Case Division received a phone call with pertinent information regarding the missing victims from author Robert Algeri.

What law enforcement decides to do with that information is their prerogative.

To the victims who fell, I have tried my best. May God rest your souls.

Heartfelt thanks to Evan Swensen of Publication Consultants and all my supporters and readers.

Do not construe any of what follows as being factual.

Robert Hansen's Malignant Shadow

Lightning bolts brightly flash above tall buildings accompanied by a chorus of sirens ringing in the background. Foreboding waves of fear shudder across W 4th Avenue in Anchorage, Alaska, because moral wickedness and corruption are sweeping this way.

With an overwhelming feeling that bad things are about to happen, people scatter into any open doorway they can find. Sullen shop keepers are quickly locking their doors and nervously pulling down dusty blinds.

A lone raven sits on top of a nearby light pole watching all this activity with curious amusement. His shiny black feathers are being bristled by the stiff breeze swirling around his head. He tilts his head left, with a lonely squawk, the raven croaks his kraa against the strong gusts of the blowing wind.

The monster of 4th Avenue has arrived, and the beast is hungry tonight.

PROLIFIC ALASKAN SERIAL KILLER ROBERT HANSEN

I am quoting a former Alaska ADA.

"Human conduct that's not human. An extreme aberration of a human being."

"Robert Hansen now has trophies scattered throughout South Central Alaska. And while he doesn't talk about it or admit to it, we know he hunted them like his big game animals. Chasing them and shooting them and sometimes killing them with a knife."

Robert Hansen found himself facing a real dilemma, one he had never envisioned. It was about to impede his primary modus operandi, that being the fly-out wilderness homicide.

In early May of 1981, the Pentagon launched a Cold War psyche-op initiative in remote northern areas of the United States that intended to lure Brezhnev out of hiding. Some people call it saber-rattling.

During this period, when the military in Alaska went on FAS, Full Alert Status, the entire airspace north of

Anchorage went into a lockdown mode. Permission to access and utilize the airspace over Elmendorf AFB and Fort Richardson, Alaska, was needed. This operation ended in late May 1983.

Robert Hansen would have needed to apply for permission to enter the airspace, thereby leaving a written record of his flight dates. It also took time to receive.

Robert Hansen needed a contingency plan, a backyard playground to commit his torture, rape, and homicides. Somewhere he could drive to, somewhere on the forgotten edge of the wilderness. Approximately four and a half miles from his house at Old Harbor Avenue, he found that ideal location in an area known as Arctic Valley.

Like a moth attracted to the fire, roaring flames of rage lure us over the hill and around the bend into the sunset for one last dance together. Bound and gagged, tied securely to a lawn wagon, then dragged for a rough ride along a dusty powerline trail by a growling homicidal maniac.

CHAPTER ONE:

BLUE TARP COVERING A MERCEDES BENZ

While looking at a map found in Robert Hansen's home, an Alaska State Trooper (AST) Detective asks Robert Hansen, "How many women, sir, have you killed in Alaska?"

Robert Hansen replies, "There are a lot of marks here. I'm going to be very honest about this. These marks represent something that they do."

I am quoting Robert Hansen, "Putting them down as lower than myself. After some time, I am back uptown. Merciless while looking again. Like a moth drawn to the fire or whatever light, I'm back again. It scared me."

Robert Hansen's embers of terror cast malignant shadows throughout the valley. While he feared no evil, fear and evil excited him. He was an abusive barbarian, invasive like a malicious and infectious epidemic. He was cryptic and callous, casting curses across his many graves.

CHAPTER TWO

MAESTRO GREENLIGHTS THE STREET'S
FOR WILDLIFE MOUNTS

Invasive rattling at the bedroom door evaporates my thought process, "Who is it?"

"Stiletto, you have a phone call waiting for you downstairs," shouts Corporal Connor through the locked door. "You have two minutes to get down there and answer it, or I will disconnect the call on you, soldier."

Slowly opening my door, I cautiously look both ways up and down the hallway. No danger is in sight. I remembered meeting a girl recently in downtown named Angie Altman. Could this be her calling me? Please let this be Angie. I need to hear her voice today.

A harsh voice resonating in my ear shakes me from my daydream, "Stiletto, how soon can you get downtown to meet with us, man?"

"Huh? Who is this? Who am I speaking with?" I respond.

"It's Dragonfly Little Monkey. I need your help with something," he replies.

"Dragonfly? What do you need me to help you with?" I ask.

"I will explain it better when we see you. Are you available to come downtown right now and meet with us?"

"No. Can you drive out to Fort Richardson and meet me next to the MP station located at the front gate?" I ask him.

"Are you kidding me, Stiletto? Are you going to make me come to you? Let me ask Maestro how he wants to handle this. Give me a minute, kid. He is outback right now."

I hear him barking out an order at Rat, "Hey, low life, do me a favor, go get Maestro so that I can speak with him; hurry up."

Pressing the phone tightly to my ear, I can hear the indistinct sound of several people speaking while I wait. Corporal Connor is standing in front of me, urgently holding up one finger while trying to signal me that my phone time is coming to an end.

The voice gets back on the phone, "Yeah, okay, I can head north now, sit tight by the MP shack until I get there. We need to go to Eagle River and see a friend of ours," he says.

"I'll be waiting for you," I reply.

When I step outside from the barracks, my face gets smacked by a blustery wind. I see a large flock of ravens floating high in the wind drafts above the power utility plant located in Arctic Valley. They took up residence there in the early spring, and now they won't leave.

Dragonfly is just getting to the front gate when it starts to rain. The MP's wave his car through and allow him to pick me up at the turnaround. The wind is whipping large pelts of water against my face, so I tilt my head back to take a drink while he unlocks the car door for me.

"Get in Stiletto, let's go," he urges me. "Hurry up, man, please. We need to fly."

"Wow, talk about some wind and rain. I agree, let's, get out of here," I respond.

Driving north on the Glenn Highway for about six miles, we exit at Artillery Rd in Eagle River, merging with the Old Glenn Highway. We continue driving for about a half mile to the corner of Easy St. We stop in front of 11723 Old Glenn Highway. Dragonfly parks the car in front of a hair salon named Sensational Cutz.

Dragonfly shoots me a scary look and says, "There was a saying back in the day in the neighborhood that I grew up as a part of Stiletto, it goes something like this, 'if you do good, we'll take care of you, if you do bad, we'll take care of you.'"

Laughing at his anecdote, I respond, "So, no matter what, you will take care of us?"

"Damn straight, Little Monkey," he replies. "Now, let's go inside and see my friend Joanne. I'll show you what I mean. Just observe, don't do any talking in here."

He continues to explain, "Joanne has become a disloyal tramp. Her husband owns a taxidermy shop in Chugiak that accommodates some high-value wildlife mounts. She was supposed to contact us when he was traveling out of state. She didn't act per our arrangement."

Not sure what Dragonfly is saying to me, I speak up, "Fly, give me the big picture so that I can get on board with the mission."

Dragonfly spins in his seat and grabs me by my shirt collar. While tightly twisting the cloth against my trachea, he pins my neck against the headrest with his muscular forearm, "Please don't make me have to kill you, Little Monkey. I love you, man. We have a guy, this friend of ours, who we partially pay with wildlife mounts."

Fragmented and incoherent thoughts are twisting inside my head when I ask, "What are you paying him to do? Why would you threaten to kill me over wildlife mounts?"

With bared teeth and an aggressive growl, he retorts, "Maestro will explain that part of the game to you when the time comes, not right now. I need you to know this. It's a deadly game we are all playing. Stay focused, or Maestro will have me put you down."

"I mean it, Stiletto. Listen to the words coming from my mouth. This is a game of death; no fooling around anymore out here. Understood?"

CHAPTER THREE

DAMON DIRKS THE KIDNAPPER AND HUMAN TRAFFICKER

Fairview Neighborhood, Anchorage, Alaska 1980

"Hey, Sally, h-h-how are you doing today? Is your mother expecting you home anytime soon?" My voice quietly coaxes her toward the idling truck. She gently nods her head yes to my question while slowly approaching me.

"Yes, Mr. Dirks, she is waiting for me to come home right now," Sally replies.

"Let's surprise your mother; I can help you get home quicker. Jump in on the other side, and I will drive you home right away," I gently prod her.

I wait while she thinks about it, smiling; she decides to run around the back of my truck and comes up along the side toward the passenger door. I start frantically scanning my mirrors to see if anyone is watching us. My heart is thundering in my chest as she reaches for the door handle. I can hear her soft, childish voice ringing in my ears.

"Mr. Dirks, my mother is going to be upset with me for getting a ride from you. I am not supposed to get into anyone else's car," she sternly proclaims.

"That's nonsense, Sally. W-w-we go way back, your family and mine, so now be a good girl, jump in, and let's get going," I retort.

As soon as she gets in, I smother her with a pillowcase. As she desperately struggles with me, I wrestle her hands under control by handcuffing her to a bar I have secured to my center console. Her ferocious screams are muffled by the pillowcase I have pulled over her head. I wrap duct tape around her shoulders to help keep it in place over her upper body.

"Calm down, S-S-Sally. If you do what I need you to do, everything will go good for you," I try to assure her. I attempt to rub her head, but she pulls back, shrieking, "I hate you, Mr. Dirks!"

I try to stay calm while meandering across midtown Anchorage toward my meeting location with Dragonfly, but my mind is in a flurry. *Should I buy a new pair of hunting boots? Maybe I should fix the cracks in the bakery foundation outback? What happens if Dragonfly tries to bargain me down again? Can I drop my price for him?*

We always meet over by the Old Seward Highway, down near Furrow Creek. There's a gravel road that takes us to a little clearing. It's the contact location we have been using. This girl will be heading to Honolulu, where she will get loaded on a private plane that will fly her to Miami. After Miami, her final destination will be South

Africa. Once she arrives there, she will be hunted by members of the transnational elite.

Slowly inching my truck up next to Dragonfly's orange taxi cab, I glance over at him and casually nod my head. He responds by beeping his horn and pounding on his steering wheel. He is red-faced.

Jumping out of his taxi, he yells, "Dirks, you better have something good for us. You are forty minutes late," while his baseball mitt-size hand is trembling to get a cigarette out of its package.

Shaking his head, he continues, "Dirks, you better not have dipped your fingers? Did you Dirks? Please tell me no, Dirks? Did you touch this girl at all?"

Shaking my head no, I respond, "Dragonfly I-I-I came quickly."

He retorts, "Yeah, I bet you did. You're a wet daydream, Dirks. Bring me the merchandise. What a freak show you are. A complete departure from what is normal," he taunts.

Sally has finally stopped screaming, but she is crying uncontrollably. It's a little struggle wrestling her from my truck and getting her over to Dragonfly's taxi cab, but my pay is well worth the fight. She will fulfill someone's ultimate sexual bondage hunting fantasy.

After we complete the exchange, Dragonfly gets into my truck to pay me. "Here you are, Dirks. As promised. Thirty-two, one-ounce South African gold Krugerrands and a bear rug wall mount worth approximately seven-thousand dollars. That's about twenty-five thousand dollars in street value. Are we good, Dirks?"

Sullenly I respond, "Yes, totally good. I thought you would be happier?"

"Happy? Happy to meet with you? Under these conditions? Listen, Dirks keep the salmon running twenty-four hours a day out here. Understood? This is a job for me. I am not your friend."

Dragonfly is on a rant as he continues to light me up, "I can't stand you, Dirks. Give me one reason to bury you. You are a degenerate psychopath. You better stay on track. Keep it squared away out here, or I will be coming to get you."

"You let me pull out of here before you do. Stay right here for at least fifteen minutes before you leave," his raspy voice continues to drone on, buzzing in the background like a fly. Why have I become involved with these guys? How long can this carry on? I keep thinking to myself.

CHAPTER FOUR

DAMON DIRKS PROLIFIC SERIAL KILLER NOTORIOUS LIAR

I always seem to find myself back uptown here, like a moth attracted to the fire or whatever light, the corner of Denali Street and W 4th Avenue, Anchorage, Alaska. Mount Denali is known as the great one—the tallest mountain in North America. *Am I king of the mountain now? Have I become the most wicked wolf in this valley? Was I preordained for all this lust?*

This sexy girl over here caught my attention. I am intrigued by her red high heels. Let me casually pull over. I don't want to spook her in any way. Toot the horn, give her a gentle head nod, put my turn signal on. I want to take it easy and relax.

Nice, she noticed my signals. Her head swivels scanning, both ways before walking toward my truck. I roll my window down so I can speak with her, "Hey, y-y-you going out tonight?" I calmly ask her. She nods her head yes while coyly leaning against my passenger door.

"Are you looking for a good time, honey? What can Starr do for you tonight? You're not a cop, are you?" I nod no. She continues, "I can give it all to you for two hundred dollars. Would that work for you, honey? You get the complete package and a whole lot of love."

"That works for me. Get in," I retort. Starr seems relieved, maybe even surprised in a way that I have excepted her price without haggling. As soon as she gets in, I back fist her with my revolver. I like hearing the crunching sound against her teeth. Her hands instinctively go up, attempting to protect her face allowing me to get a handcuff around her left wrist. I quickly connect her to the security bar attached to my center console. She starts screaming.

"Don't kill me! Are you the guy? Are you the guy?" she is frantic. Realization sets in, her lips start quivering uncontrollably. "I hate you!" she cries. "Why me?"

"Shut up over there. Calm down. Do as I say, and everything will go good for you. We are going to do this a little differently tonight," I explain to her.

"You are a professional. You have been practicing this activity for a while. Stay quiet. It will all be over soon," I assure her.

Like a lot of activities, hunting is all about location. Choosing good ground and being in the right place at the right time becomes all-important for a successful hunt, no matter what the prey is. With humans, it is no different.

Once I am on Arctic Valley Road near the Doyon utility plant, I realize the brightening of the night sky from the power facility lights. It has a disruptive effect that creates light pollution, helping conceal my roaring fires from curious or inquiring eyes.

The electrical humming of the power plant's generator system drowns out the women's horrendous screaming.

After I kill them, I leave wind chimes resonating along the treeline. The metallic cadence from the wind chimes helps keep curious predators at bay. Skittish with fear, they tend to move on without investigating the smell of any flesh decay.

If the kill is good and promises to provide tender meat, sometimes I crave that sweet taste followed by slightly bitter aftertaste. The aroma of seared flesh in my nostrils sends me howling into the moonless night like a victorious wolf stomping.

CHAPTER FIVE

ALASKA STATE TROOPER DETECTIVE HILDEBRANDT INTERVIEWS SERIAL KILLER DAMON DIRKS

I am beginning to realize that my ultimate fantasy seems to be punishing bad girls who look to exchange sex for money. Have I gone blindly insane?

Impatiently, Detective Hildebrandt inquires, "Are we ready to bring Dirks in for his interrogation, Sergeant?"

"Yes, sir. We are ready." I can't begin to imagine what must be going through Detective Hildebrandt's head right now. He has been incessantly working on this case for years. His tenacity is a thing of admiration among the ranks.

With finely tuned surgical precision, the armed escort with Damon Dirks marches toward me. They have him shackled in chains. He looks disheveled at best. As is usual with Dirks, he seems to be pulling back, skulking within the shadow.

Do these cops think they are going to beat and break me? They can give me no protection from Maestro or Dragonfly.

I am in fear of severe bodily harm or death for myself. My family is at extreme risk. If Maestro finds out how many exotic dancers I have kidnapped and murdered, my two children will have to face the dire consequences waiting for them overseas.

Did Stiletto recognize me that night on Denali St? Does he recognize me from all the security stops up in Arctic Valley? Will he remember throwing me out of the Wild Cherry that Sunday afternoon? What happens if he finally pieces all of this together?

He is the only person who has seen and interacted with me in all of these locations. Maestro introduced us at his home during a cocktail party one night. He's been to my bakery numerous times, that's a problem for me.

Look at this son of a bitch Hildebrandt over here. He looks like a walking hard-on. Maybe I can ask Stiletto to send Dragonfly over to Hildebrandt's house, kidnap, and embed his wife in the treacherous waters of the chilly Cook Inlet for me. That would teach him.

Hildebrandt speaks first, "Damon, I am hoping today is the day you decide to do the right thing for our community here in Anchorage? Do the right thing for your family Damon, for the families of the missing victims."

Hissing, I respond, "What do you know about my family? What's right for my family detective? I have always done the right thing."

Hildebrandt retorts, "The right thing? Are you kidding me, Dirks? You have confessed to killing at least seventeen people? Seriously? The right thing?"

Before I can respond, Hildebrandt continues with his verbal tirade, "Dirks you little—little man. Your only power now is protecting this knowledge, this dirty little secret of yours. Oh, look at me. I am Damon Dirks. I am the big bad wolf. Is that how it goes here, Damon?"

Trembling, gritting teeth, my fists clenched, I yell at him, "Never! Never detective. You will never figure this out. No location, no dead bodies. That's my final answer."

Who does Dirks think he is? Does he believe he is a werewolf? Am I supposed to surrender here? Concede to him? Just throw in the towel? What about all the missing victims and their families? Should I announce my retirement from law enforcement?

CHAPTER SIX:

Alaska State Trooper Detective Hildebrandt Interviews Damon Dirks Grandaughter

Detective Hildebrandt looks sad. "Good morning Henrietta. Thank you for volunteering to come here today and answer some of our questions about your grandfather Damon Dirks."

Before I can respond to the detective, he continues, "If you need to stop this process at any time, please feel the liberty to do so. We are only here because of your willingness to answer some tough questions. I am sure this will be an emotional drain for you."

I respond, "Detective, I am trying to help you locate all the missing women. I have been agonizing while driving around Anchorage recently, studying maps, hoping to find a lost clue."

"Henrietta, this must be an extremely tough circumstance for you; your family is broke and humiliated. Your grandfather incarcerated," Hildebrandt replies.

"Detective, you have no idea. Lots of times I get these appalling images in my head, I need to rinse them from my mind."

It was a long time ago, maybe in late 1978, my mom had to quickly and unexpectedly drop me off at my grandfather's house over near Muldoon. When we arrived, she scolded me to hurry up and get inside. It was snowing lightly. Waving to the ghost of her disappearing station wagon as it rolled down the driveway, I turned and started walking to the front door of my grandfather's house.

What is that growling noise? My grandfather doesn't own a dog. Does he know I am at his front door? Why hasn't he answered my knocks yet? Is that a wolf I hear howling?

Every muscle in my body tightened. I decided to try and creep alongside the house silently. I stopped and peered intently through a steamy basement window when I came to it. I was instantly horrified yet strangely intrigued by what I was seeing.

My eyes were resting on a naked woman chained by her neck to a splintery wooden post. The woman's tears had streaked clumps of mascara all over her bruised cheeks. She slumped in despair, quivering like a leaf fluttering against a harsh autumn wind.

My grandfather was also naked. When I saw him, I felt a tremor of white heat pulse through my bosom. My grandfather was ritualistically dancing naked while mocking the sobbing lady. He seemed to be gyrating to a broken beat within his head.

Detective Hildebrandt looks frightened. His eyes widen in disbelief as he begins to understand my words,

"Henrietta, we have long suspected that your grandfather had a co-conspirator from among law enforcement or the military ranks. Did you ever observe these types of people at his home during any of your visits?"

"No, I did not. No, never," I reply.

Hildebrandt squirms at my response. He seems to be struggling to maintain his resolve, "Henrietta, do you think your grandfather ever thought of not murdering his victims, having his way with them, but then releasing and letting them go?"

"Oh, no, he would have never released any of them. He just wanted to amuse himself. He wanted them to grovel for their freedom so he could tell them no."

Is Is Henrietta Damon Dirks co-conspirator? Could he be that malicious? How far did Dirks go with all this? Should I go shoot him now?

CHAPTER SEVEN:

ARE YOU YOUR BROTHER'S KEEPER DE LUCIANO?

May 1981, jumping from a slow-moving jeep, I have just received orders to walk three miles through thick stands of devil's club, trailblazing my way to a forward observation post in the Chugach Mountains. Wielding a machete in my hand, I trudge upward. Below me, I can hear Ship Creek flowing from the mountains. I am alone in the thick shrubbery of South Central Alaska when my mind begins to dwell on the possibility of dire circumstances falling on me.

Later that night, as if in a dream, I can hear the echoing shouts of a terrified woman rising from below me. She is desperate with her pleas. At first, I pass it off. It can't be real. There's no one up here other than me. As her shrieks continue, I decide to explore the shouting that seems to be rolling up from the valley below. Nobody will believe me.

"Who gave you permission to raise your ugly head De Luciano? Why do you care so much about this particular circumstance? Let their families deal with it all. You are an asset to the US Army. They are not. Let the dead collect and bury their dead, now stand down."

I retort, "Yes sir General Masanotti." *No way, this can't be real? Am I real? Is this reality?* I look like a fool. No one believes me. Stand down?

I can still feel the horror resonating across the valley, mysteriously menacing with a gripping ferocity. There was something sinister in the atmosphere up there.

CHAPTER EIGHT:

CID DEPORTS ANTHONY DE LUCIANO, THE STILETTO, FROM ALASKA

*N*PD. *Is no pay due?* Why has this happened to me? I feel like I am standing back in No Man's Land, thrashing in quicksand while grasping for the overhanging branch of a cottonwood tree. I can feel the sand's grip, pulling on me like the torrent current of a raging creek as it spews my limp and rag-like body into muddy- and silt-clouded Cook Inlet. My severe mental suffering to understand who I am is billowing in my head.

Driving through the Government Hill, neighborhood of Anchorage, Alaska, from the back entrance of Elmendorf Air Force Base, CID has chained me in a steel cage inside the cold cabin of an Army Green Transport Van that is windowless. They have put a Kevlar face muzzle on me to keep me from directing verbal insults at them.

The military has three highly trained escorts guarding me. Each person is camouflaged and heavily armed with knives, sidearms, and long guns. They casually announce to me that they also have stun guns available, if needed. We engage in a riveting and dizzying drive across the windswept city of Anchorage.

I can still hear General Masanotti's voice inside my head as he was relieving me of my duties. "De Luciano, you have disappointed the US Army; with your insistence that we shift directive and engage in law enforcement activities. You are not your brother's keeper unless I give you a direct order to do so. You were asked to stand down repeatedly."

What made me think I could fight city hall standing by myself? How could I take on what's known as this man's army? Have I gone completely insane? I just destroyed a promising military career with my disrespectful behavior. I have become a disgrace to my uniform. I shamed my country. I have lost the right to look at my fellow citizens in their eyes. Line up the firing squad and take me out back to shoot me now.

Our driver violently slams the brakes on. The surge of my body weight against the wrist restraints brings intense stinging, like needles of pain. My eyes are watering from the pain. I can see two shadowy figures waiting by the door as we pull up next to it. It looks like they are both holding shotguns. One of my escorts exits the vehicle, and I watch as paperwork gets exchanged between the two shadowy figures.

A back door to the building opens up, and a burly woman steps from the shadow. She opens a small black case and removes a little vial full of brown-yellowish powder. She motions toward one of the men holding the door open, and he hands her a water container. While she pours the powder into the water container and shakes it up, she speaks with me.

"My name is Special Agent Kittie Hawk. This is a mild sedative we are going to administer to you. It will keep you from making any rash decisions once you are up in the air. We will be removing your restraints for the flight from Anchorage, Alaska to Seattle, Washington. Enjoy your flight, PFC De Luciano." With a smile, she pushes the needle in, "Oh, now dream on my friend," she mumbles.

Shackled, humiliated, and bouncing between two heavily built guards, they escort me through an unlit rear entrance of the Anchorage International Airport. A large clock on the wall reads 11:42 P.M. I get shoved into a dimly lit hallway with a 50Hz hum that is disgusting and painful to my eyes. The flicker of the light causes me to squint and overwhelms me with an urge to vomit.

As we approach the plane's door, we meet two official-looking people, one is a woman, and she has a male partner at her side. She is the leader and her male partner looks like a lost deer with his legs buckling across the pavement in the headlights. The woman flashes a badge and states her name to my escorts, "I am Special Agent Veronica Sage. My partner is Special Agent Walt Hickman. We will take the detainee from here."

Veronica Sage looks stern. Walt Hickman has a gloomy appearance. I have a feeling of being perplexed and confused as they remove my muzzle and restraints. Sage barks out several orders, "Keep your back away from this guy, and keep him in front of you at all time." I am finding it comical and entertaining.

My commanding officer recently informed me that the government had spent US$330,000 for training me over the last two and a half years. Now I am nothing but a reviled beast to them, cast about like a shaggy dog, forced to drink from a bowl of his vomit. Agent Hickman sneers at me, "De Luciano, give me any good reason to put you in a hole in the ground tonight."

Our planes hop off the back tarmac is smooth. The agents have left me standing in the service-port area of the cabin. I notice there is no support crew flying with us. Onboard we have two pilots, two special agents, and myself, Anthony De Luciano, a.k.a., the Stiletto, a.k.a., Little Monkey. I find it rather ominous that I am on a private flight to the States with no other passengers.

When the pilot removes the seat-belt sign and announces we are at altitude, Veronica Sage marches into my personal space and confronts me. "De Luciano, we are giving you the freedom of full access to the entire cabin; feel free to sit wherever you choose."

Agent Sage continues speaking with me, "We appreciate your service to the United States over the last two and a half years; now I would like to request that you treat us with professional courtesy tonight and allow us to have a peaceful journey?"

Now I am confused? How can they appreciate my service? Is this appreciation? Allow us to have a peaceful journey? Why would I sabotage my flight? Will this plane make it to Seattle?

CHAPTER NINE:

VERONICA SAGE DELIVERS A SURPRISE PACKAGE

Veronica is an enticing woman. Her eyes torment you with the promise of something that's just out of your reach. When she sits down next to me, Veronica instinctively leans across my shoulder. Her warm, raspy voice is harsh in my ear, "De Luciano, I like you a lot. Why couldn't we have come into each other's lives at a more convenient time? I do have something for you. I think you are going to love what I have."

My eyes follow her strut. Her sinewy calves help her drift like she is walking on clouds. She returns carrying a military duffel bag. It is secure with a large brass lock. "De Luciano, this is courtesy of the United States Government and myself, Special Agent Veronica Sage. We would like to ask you a question, Do you accept this package under the guidelines of the United States Code of Military Justice?"

I sputter, "Ma'am? Please come again, over?" What is this lady agent saying to me? Where is agent Hickman through all this? *Will this plane arrive in the lower forty-eight safely? What kind of a test is this? Who am I becoming lately?*

She responds, "You know the drill, De Luciano. We need to hear a verbal acknowledgment coming from your mouth. Do you accept this package? Yes or no?"

I retort, "Yes, ma'am, I accept the package." With a triumphal grunt, Agent Sage tosses the duffel bag at my feet. Placing her sweaty hands-on pushed-out hips, she sternly barks, "Don't even think of opening this package until you get home. Do you understand me, De Luciano?"

Vigorously nodding my head, I respond, "Yes, I understand, no problems will come from me." What am I going to find in this bag? Is this some of the bounty money they promised me? *Is Sergeant Phillips CIA or CID? Does he know I suspect Angie's grave is in No Man's Land? I only told Dragonfly. No way, is Fly CID? Is Maestro CIA?*

CHAPTER TEN:

SEARCHING FOR ANGIE ALTMAN'S GRAVE

It was cold, and a fierce wind was blowing straight at her. A writhing silhouette dancing on the rocks enclosed by rain, sleet, and fog shimmers before me. When I reach my cold, soggy hand toward her, she disappears. I can't seem to shake Angie out of my mind.

As our car approaches the Canadian border, a soft drizzle begins to fall, and the lights from an unseen border station signal us of the perils that might lay ahead. The Oldsmobile Delta 98 grinds to a shuddering halt in front of a brightly lit building resembling a tollbooth.

Looking bored, a pugnacious woman glances into our cabin interior with stern calculating eyes. With a heavy French-Canadian accent, she shouts out, "Have either of you ever been inside of a courtroom before?"

Deciding to joke around with her, I yell back, "No, I don't gamble; I have never been inside of a cardroom before." My friend Mike starts laughing with me. The female border guard doesn't find it to be funny.

She engages me again, "Sir, have you ever been inside of a courtroom for any reason?" Her delicious Canadian accent is tugging on my heartstrings.

Gleefully I retort, "I already told you I don't gamble, no I have never been inside of a cardroom. What's going on here? We are going to Vancouver for personal business. Why are you doing this to us tonight?"

The border guard decides to ask my friend Mike if he has been drinking alcohol tonight, "Sir, have you been drinking alcohol tonight? What are you holding in your hand?"

Mike lifts his beer bottle, "I drank four already and, I have a cold one going right now."

She gets angry and snaps at us, "Pull your vehicle over now. Drive into waiting lane number five for me immediately. Please do as I have instructed you."

While we slowly inch our car forward for her, a sharply dressed police officer storms from inside the main building. He lunges into a verbal tirade directed at several young border guards standing off to his left. They all look our way and start running toward our car.

A horn begins to sound, rotating lights are flashing, and the female border guard begins blowing her whistle with extreme force—a melee of uniformed bodies swarms around our car. One of the guards is red-faced and screaming at me, "Are you an American gangster? Sir, are you an American gangster? Answer me."

Disorientated by what I am finding to be inappropriate and disturbing behavior from our Canadian friends, I blurt out, "I am an American friend of yours going to Vancouver for pleasure. I am looking for my lost girlfriend.

She called me recently and asked me to come and visit her in your city."

Spewing venom, one of the guards shouts back, "Nonsense, you are a gangster! Why are you coming into our country to start trouble tonight? Please exit the vehicle with your hands up," he orders us.

In a blur of hands, five people reach for their sidearms at the same time. Exasperated by their disrespectful behavior, we oblige them by pushing our hands to the sky. After grudgingly stepping from the safety of our car, they escort us to the inside of a dreadful building.

Two tough-looking guards roughly segregate me away from Mike and shove me into a small office, afterward slamming the door tight behind them. The room is bland. It has no furnishings except for a small desk with three chairs tattered along the edge. Stunned by this comedic turn of events, I sullenly take a seat in one of the shabby chairs.

The sound of broken shouts coming from outside the cheap door, accompanied by heavy footsteps stomping toward the office, causes me to face the door. My stomach clenches, a sharp rattling shakes the door as a crisply dressed police officer steps into the room. He brings with him a sense of superiority.

The officer immediately launches into a scorching verbal tirade, "Do you know who I am? I am the Commandant of British Columbia. I am in charge of the whole border for the entire province."

Prancing before me with a swelled chest, he attempts to regale me, "I control the entire border of British

Columbia. Do you know Ze-Rule gangster? I asked you if you know Ze-Rule American gangster?"

My thoughts are outside of this room, dwelling on a particular girl. His words are swirling around inside my head. I can hear him shouting Ze-Rule, Ze-Rule, over and over again. Incessant shouting finally shakes me back into the office, "Huh? Ze-Rule?" I retort.

Before he can respond, I continue, "Listen to me, Commandant, I am not an American gangster. No, I do not know Ze-Rule, okay? What's this all about? Why are you hassling me tonight?"

Enraged and red-faced, he screams, "Don't you come into my country asking me the questions? I ask all the questions, understood? I make Ze-Rule!" He jumps up and violently kicks an empty chair in my direction before storming out of the office.

Maneuvering back into the office like a rabid commando, the Commandant heaves a massive three-ring binder onto the desk. Muttering under his breath, he opens it up. He is overflowing with rage. His bony finger violently jabs down at the page.

He demands, "Look and read what I am saying. This is Ze-Rule! Read it!"

I kid you not in print it read, "Ze-Rule." In general, it was stating that the Commandant has sole authority to make, suspend, or deviate from any law, rule, or guideline to enforce the law according to their needs. Sullenly I look up at him.

He is gleeful when he proclaims, "We are not in America, you are in a sovereign Fascist country. In my country, you have no rights unless I say so. I will not tolerate American garbage coming into my country, Gangster, go home!" he spits onto the carpet for emphasis.

Katherine calls out to me from the shadow, eager to help me find Angie's grave. I can see a tear in her undies, frayed and uneven. As we begin dancing in a hallway full of mirrors, light is refracting across the surface of the floor.

CHAPTER ELEVEN:

ANTHONY TRACKS DOWN KATHERINE IN VANCOUVER, B.C.

I dreamed of a girl standing next to me, and now she is gone, with subtle gestures, her scent full of aromatic stimulation lingering in the air. I can see her silhouetted behind the flame. Sweet dreams are clouding my mind.

Unsettling but captivating thoughts have flooded my mind since I decided to leave my job at the Bright Angel Lodge near the Grand Canyon in Arizona. I feel like someone has been standing behind me, watching. At the same time, I yearn for that person to catch up with me. *Is this Katherine looking for me? How can I expect her to remember me? Why would she like me? Has this all been for nothing? Am I crazy?*

The woman behind the glass is glaring at me, "Excuse me, Sir, I have asked you three times if you need my assistance tonight?" My stomach performs a flip, and my eyes widen with confusion as I respond to her.

"Yes, would you please direct me to the proper train for Vancouver," my thoughts are about love and fate? Strange, eerie, and terrifying thoughts start to ooze and surge through me.

"What is the first and last name of the person traveling?" The woman asks me.

"My name is Anthony De Luciano," I reply.

The acrid smell of stale tobacco reeking from the teller lady reaches my nose. I can't help feeling lost, mildly confused. Am I searching for a lost cause?

What are you doing to yourself this time, Anthony? Why are you going to Vancouver? Are you looking for trouble? Are you going insane?

Crazy or not here, I come. My train is traveling at a high rate of speed. Looking from the window, I watch as sparks of lightning illuminate the rain. I find it electrifying and riveting to try and count the raindrops before they splatter against my foggy window.

My shuddering train slowly approaches the city limits of Vancouver. We disembark onto a slippery and windswept platform, surrounded by the dark, icy waters of Mitchell Island.

My taxi driver's name is Trae. He is highly skilled at driving in the rain. Trae uses a clenched fist to shift his car as we navigate the fog-enclosed shore. Ninjutsu is an ancient and rare martial art system, Katherine, is the most proficient practitioner, the most skilled in its wily ways. She owns a small martial arts studio along the Fraser River at Rue Cherrier and Eburne Way.

As we sharply veer around a curve, Trae informs me his nickname is the prince of darkness. "Hey, I am known as the prince of darkness around here." He gives me a curious glance in his rearview mirror while watching for my reaction.

Hesitating, I reply, "Nice to meet you, Mr. Prince of Darkness," as my body stiffens.

Trae continues, "Do you want to know why they call me the prince of darkness?" while he is reaching over to turn up his radio, "Do you like listening to music?" he asks.

I can hear a raspy voice singing about sympathy for the devil, languishing about wealth and taste, loudly coming from the radio, "Please allow me to introduce myself. I am a man of wealth and taste," Trae starts tapping his fingers along the steering wheel, "So if you meet me, have some courtesy, some sympathy, and some taste."

Trae looks back at me intently over his right shoulder, "That's the Rolling Stones singing that song right there my friend. Have you ever worshipped the devil?" he asks me.

Nodding my head no, I reply, "I only worship the goddess of reason. She is a lover of light and beauty. That is why I am here in Vancouver. I am looking for a friend that can lead me to her. My friend's name is Katherine." Without warning, Trae slams his brakes on, causing us to skid wildly on top of the slippery pavement. With a jolt, the car comes to a stop on the shoulder of the road.

Grimacing in horror at me, Trae screams, "Get out now! Get out! Out of my vehicle right now!" while pointing his trembling finger back at me. He continues his tirade as I hurriedly exit from his car. As the door is slamming shut, I can hear him yelling, "Katherine is nothing but a brazen bitch."

I shake my head in disbelief while his spinning tires splash cold water back on me. Watching as his car disappears in a dizzying array of red light, I am paralyzed and overwhelmed with a feeling of impending danger.

Katherine was supposed to be here, keeping her head down and staying out of trouble.

Has Katherine been creating drama? Should I continue over to her house? What happens if it's dangerous? Does Katherine need my help?

CHAPTER TWELVE:

FATE FINDS KATHERINE WAITING

One thing everyone I've talked with agrees upon, even as a baby, Katherine liked spicy food. I am hoping this means she will be open-minded to my way of thought. I am a person who has derived my style from a broad and diverse range of sources. Call it eclectic taste.

From an early age, I have learned a lethal combination of stick and knife fighting skills. I have learned to take the shape of my container, which makes me a potent counter-fighter. I move with an unsteady, broken rhythm while dancing to an unheard beat.

Upon my approach to Katherine's front door, I can hear loud music coming from inside her home. Will she be able to hear me knocking? Before my scarred fist reaches the door panel to knock, the door is pulled wide open. Katherine jumps into my arms while shouting, "Anthony babe!" Her soft lips push tightly against mine.

Katherine's embrace is firm as she spins me around and pushes us both up against the wall. I tremble convulsively.

I am feeling dizzy and weak as my stomach begins to twist. A blustery wind clutches at Katherine's satin robe, swirling it around our entwined legs.

When I turn to face her, Katherine kisses me again. A silent howl erupts from within the wolf's throat. Her fur tickles my tender skin. Wild fondling occurs, with lively stomping our tectonic thunder emblazons us with a shuddering climax.

Giggling, we both start laughing in a silly way, "Can you believe we just had sex on your front walkway?" I ask her in disbelief. Katherine nestles her head firmly into my chest.

She looks up at me. Tears have streaked her eyes. Pushing out of my embrace, she stumbles backward, "You searched for me until you found me. I have never been pursued with such a devoted effort. My insides are on fire. I feel like I am melting."

I reply, "Katherine, my heart has been frozen in time waiting for this exact moment. There are only two things that matter to me in this life, you and finding the location of Angie's grave. I need you in my life, Katherine. I will love you until the end of time."

"What do we need to do?" she asks me.

"We must return to Anchorage as soon as possible. I have enough money to get us started. A good friend of mine has already put some things in motion for us, but we need to act quickly," Katherine silently nods her approval.

We find ourselves on the next train to Whitehorse, Yukon Territory, Canada. A friend of mine then drives us across Route 1 to the Alaskan border, where we merge onto Route 2 over to Tetlin Junction, Alaska. We finally arrive at a hidden location.

Chapter Thirteen:

Rendezvous at Tetlin Junction, Alaska

Glowing from a red lantern, light splashes across the snow-covered driveway as we pull into Veronica's cabin. Katherine is clutching my hand. Our driver is succinct with her communications. "We are here," she announces.

Before we exit the vehicle, we watch as two young bull moose stride across the front lawn. We have mountain ash trees growing all around us. It is a favorite browse for moose, so they frequent this area once the fruit starts to ripen.

We walk around back to the underground bunker. It's been years since I have been here. Veronica is waiting for us, and she is not alone. Sitting within the shadows, but not blind to what's happening in the room, we see a man with cold-steel, blue eyes. It's Maestro.

Maestro? Does Veronica know Maestro? What's going on here? My heart is thundering in my ears. Katherine looks concerned. Her voice is low, and her eyes seem to be blazing holes through my bowed head. "What's happening here, Anthony? Who is this man? Explain."

Maestro speaks up, "I'll explain. Stiletto, nice to see you again, Little Monkey. Are you going to introduce me to your lady friend?"

I respond, "Maestro, meet Katherine. We met at Club Paris restaurant in Anchorage one evening while she was working as a waitress. Katherine, this is Maestro, my former employer and a friend of mine from Anchorage."

Both of us sit down. Veronica seems disengaged, she is standing over near the wood-burning stove, but she's wearing her sidearm. At the moment, this isn't looking good.

Maestro speaks up, "Stiletto, you have seen a lot of things. You know a lot of things. People have entrusted you with high levels of information. I am sure you have started to see the bigger picture of what you were involved with back in Anchorage."

Mildly confused by this turn of events, I retort, "Seriously, Maestro, you bring me here to blow smoke up my rear end? Is this your version of a joke? They caged me and tried to banish me from Alaska! Why didn't you step in and stop the charade? I never turned on any of you guys."

Feeling unleashed, I let my tirade continue, "As much as possible, I followed orders every step of the way. I never blurred the lines with you guys. Every crime I witnessed, I was willing to stop or report. It was you and CID that stopped me from fully engaging."

Maestro jumps up and storms toward me, "Are you implying I am CID Stiletto?" he screams. "Are you saying right here, right now that I am CID?" He is infuriated. His sputtering continues, "I should snap your neck right here, you little worm."

Veronica Sage has her hand on her pistol. She appears ready to shoot me at any time. The veins in my neck are throbbing. Katherine is agitated, trying to maintain her resolve not to become involved.

CHAPTER FOURTEEN

MAESTRO SUGGESTS AN UNDERTAKING FOR STILETTO

Katherine explodes, "I demand to know what is happening here? Now, would someone please explain this to me?" She is visibly trembling with anger. Her rosy cheeks betray her fury as she shoots me a disgusted look over her left shoulder. "Anthony? Veronica?"

Maestro raises his hand, trying to console her, "Katherine, I know this is confusing for you. Anthony is good at his job. I can now see that he never told you much about his job at all. Dragonfly told me when you two first met, once I realized you were good for Stiletto, we let the relationship continue."

Maestro barks out an order toward Veronica, "Sage, go get my backpack. Grab the bottle of cognac from the front pocket, pour Katherine and yourself a drink." He motions for me to follow him outside. I can hear him muttering under his breath, "Damn cold up here."

When we get outside, Maestro grabs me by the neck and kisses my forehead. His slobbering lips leave a streak of saliva, "I am so glad you decided to come back, Little Monkey. I need your expertise in the field. I have a problem. You may have a problem."

He continues, "You know they arrested Dirks for the murders of the exotic dancers and prostitutes? We had eyes on him, as you are well aware. It was only a matter of time before someone got to him. I was able to pull some strings from behind the scenes that kept him in prison this time."

At this point, I feel the need to speak up and ask questions, "Maestro, are you CIA? I want to know the scope of what I am dealing with. Is Katherine in any danger? How do you know Veronica Sage?"

He retorts, "Am I CIA? Am I this, am I that? Who am I? Might I ask who you are? We can play this game all day, Stiletto. You know who I am. Leave it at that."

"I'm the guy that needs you to do something for me. Dirks was being paid in African Gold Krugerrands for some of the services that he provided me. Unbeknownst to me, he was burying some of his women with a keepsake, a little currency to help ensure their success in the afterlife."

My stomach tightens, sweat is building around my collar, "Are you asking me to locate Dirk's hidden burial ground and dig these women up?" Are you asking me to engage in grave robbing? "You are asking me to remove evidence from a crime scene. That's a big risk, Maestro."

"Stiletto, I have been informed by law enforcement at a very high level that you are an authority on Damon

Dirks. I have also been told that you may have a map of the graveyard. Is this information correct? I demand an answer right now."

Shaking my head in disbelief, "Maestro, my friend, what's it worth to you?" I ask.

Retorting, he screams, "Unbelievable Stiletto, are you asking about compensation? Is it about the money for you? How about if I promise not to kill you? Is that a fair compensation for you, Little Monkey? "You get to go home when this is over. That's your compensation package."

Some people get invited to dance with the devil just once, and most won't survive that encounter. I got invited to dance with three devils numerous times. Did I survive?

CHAPTER FIFTEEN:

MAESTRO'S LASER PRINT SHOP IN SPENARD

Maestro opens his arms, smiling. He makes a gesture with his hand encouraging me to come closer, "Stiletto, come here. Let me hug you, my friend. We need to reacquaint ourselves." His embrace seems to be genuine. The moment gets disrupted by his snarling breath, "Stiletto I, want you to meet my missing partner, Yohann Ru'desh."

"Here's how this is about to come down. You will be working with Veronica down at my new store in Anchorage. I got a piece of a business in midtown. I also have a position for Katherine if she would be willing to work for me. We sold out the building at 417 D Street and moved the operation over to 3231 Spenard Road."

Mystified, I blurt out, "What? Who is Yohann Ru'desh?"

His grin is overbearing, "Stiletto my, friend, you have an amazing insight. Come here, I love you, man." Maestro snares me up in a bear hug. His breath is like a furnace against my neck. My carotid artery twitches in response. "Forget about Yohann Ru'desh for now. Forget I mentioned him."

Pushing back out of his embrace, I stare up into his cold-steel eyes, "Look at the address Maestro, you are into basic numerology. 3231 Spenard Rd, 3 + 2 + 3 + 1 = 9. Nine represents final judgment in the Occult and Bible. I have to ask you how is this being discreet? You are telegraphing your intent to anyone with eyes that can see clearly."

Maestro snarls down at me, "There's one thing you are not taking into account here, I own this state. When you own the state, you can telegraph whatever you want to whomever you want. Is that understood? This is bigger than you step back right now."

He continues, "We are running a small laser print shop in there. We do high-resolution work for transnational elite. We print birth certificates, identifications, passports, résumés, LSAT results. If you need it, we can deliver on the promise. We are also printing currency, high-quality foreign currency."

My throat goes dry, "Currency? USSR? Japan? Transnational elite?" He starts laughing at me with no remorse.

"Stiletto you are a babe in the woods my friend. How do you think we finance all these covert operations based out of Alaska? It takes large quantities of money to operate from remote northern areas that lack material circumstances. Do you think we are panning for gold to line our pockets up here?" His laugh is becoming hurtful and malicious.

CHAPTER SIXTEEN:

PONDERING THE CONDUCT OF DAMON DIRKS

"Ladies, I have a looming problem. Maestro has just become a thorn in my side. Veronica, are you sure you want to be involved with me here?" *I feel like I am doomed, with cosmic impotence, burdened by sadistic dismay.*

Eyes wide and her mouth partially open, Veronica looks upset by my question, "Of course, I am all in the game. I have a lot of solid reasons for being here with you. Reason number one, the money is great."

I query, "What is reason number two?"

"I need to protect the toxic twins from themselves. If I leave you two alone in Anchorage, naughty things may happen," Veronica replies.

Shaking my head in disbelief, I continue, "I have a truckload of information to share, and it may seem a little disjointed at times. I appreciate all of your support and your willingness to be in this game with me to the end. Are we ready to begin?"

Katherine raises her hand, "Anthony, please tell me you are not going to help Maestro? Or are you?" Quickly shaking my head no, I respond to her question.

"No, I will not. We need to misdirect Maestro to make him believe that we are following the plan and we are on it for him. If we are successful, all my information will go to law enforcement. Then it will be theirs to deal with. We are only trying to do the right thing. It is the women and men of law enforcement's responsibility to follow up and pursue the information, not ours."

"Let's start from the beginning of my involvement. Damon Dirks faced a real dilemma as a serial killer, one that he had never envisioned. It was about to impede his primary modus operandi, that being the fly-out wilderness homicide."

"In early May of 1981, the Pentagon launched a Cold War psyche-op initiative in remote northern areas of the United States that intended to lure Brezhnev out of hiding. Some call it saber-rattling. The first live-fire missions of the Stealth Bomber were involved. It was a terrifying sight to behold."

"During this time frame, when the military in Alaska went on FAS, Full Alert Status, the entire airspace just north of Anchorage, Alaska, went into a lockdown mode. The Nike missile site located up in Arctic Valley became active. Civilian flights needed permission to access and utilize the airspace over Elmendorf AFB and Fort Richardson. That operation ended in late May 1983."

"Damon Dirks would have needed to apply for permission with the command tower at Merrill Field Airport to enter the airspace, thereby leaving a written record of his flight dates. These records could have later become evidence of his misdeeds."

"Facing this dilemma, Damon Dirks needed a contingency plan, a backyard playground to commit his torture, rape, and homicides. Somewhere he could drive to on the forgotten edge of the wilderness. I think he may have found that ideal location approximately four and a half miles from his home on Old Harbor Avenue."

Both women look stunned by the thought of these spineless perversions. Shuddering, they huddle closely together while I continue speaking with them.

"At Fort Richardson, Arctic Valley Road passes through the Moose Run Golf Course as it winds its way up into the Chugach Mountains. My platoon's mission was Alaska primary. Security for a stretch of Arctic Valley Road and the Nike missile site got assigned to us. In 1981, 1982, and early 1983 we spent a great deal of time up there."

"Ok, listen up, let's take a ten-minute break. Everyone does their thing. Convene back here in ten minutes. It's about to get heavy."

Sometimes the sun was low, almost touching the horizon in the land of the midnight sun, shouts and screams followed by sounds of crying amidst the twirling tail of an ember dragon. Something sinister was lurking in the atmosphere down below us.

CHAPTER SEVENTEEN:

THE HERMIT OF ARCTIC VALLEY DAMON DIRKS

Katherine and Veronica are huddled over by the coffee station frantically, whispering back and forth amongst themselves. When both women shyly glance my way, I motion for them to return to the debrief table.

"Let's go, ladies. Ten minutes is up," I bark out. Studiously they return and take their seats.

"When the two military bases went on FAS, we had a protocol for securing and locking down the perimeter of the fort. There was a grace period for civilians to be notified of the commencement regarding the impending live-fire exercise and to have them depart the perimeter for their safety."

"We would require an ID check, record their license plate number, and ask them why they were on, or near, Fort Richardson. I was present when we detained Damon Dirks in a small dirt parking area immediately after the Doyon utility plant on at least seven occasions. He was always parked behind a small transformer station caged within a chain-link fence and capped in barbed wire."

Veronica's hand goes up, "Did you ever see him with any tools for digging?"

I respond, "No, we did not. He always had his rifle slung over his left shoulder, and he carried a pair of binoculars. He would tell us he was glassing for Dall sheep. Some of these encounters happened at night, but it's normal for sheep hunters to glass on clear nights. From what I understand, they can see the silhouettes of the sheep on the ridgelines."

"Our suspicions about the possibility of a graveyard first came about because we observed large flocks of ravens roosting along the treeline behind the utility plant and perching along the security fence. My unit also observed the ravens staying tight to the area, which seemed to imply that there is a constant food source for them. Many times, they would be on the ground scritch scratching among the undergrowth and leaf debris."

I continue speaking with the ladies, "When we finally received permission to recon and scout the area, we sent a fireteam of three guys down to look into the situation. I was among those soldiers."

"As we begin to walk down the trail away from the transformer station, we found a large round hollow built up with huge boulders creating a retaining wall along with the banking closest to the utility plant. We found a plastic lawn wagon in there. Someone had changed the original tires to blue balloon tires from a child's toy. All of us were puzzled, thinking that maybe a bear had dragged it in there, but we could not find any teeth or claw marks on it. At that time, the closest residential home was several miles away from the area of our operation."

"We left the wagon as we found it and moved into the treeline right behind the utility plant, approximately one hundred and fifty feet off the corner of their security fence. We found a dark depression that had a large fire pit next to it. The leftover coals were thick. Our radio operator immediately made contact with our superiors up on the road. He told them we suspected that we had just found a fresh gravesite. They ordered us to continue our search along the treeline."

"The team slowly made our way along the drip edge of the treeline, and about seventy-five yards due north stumbled onto another dark depression. There was another large fire pit next to it, and the coals were very thick. We made radio contact again with our chain of command. They again ordered us to continue with our search."

"In the background, we could hear a slight metallic tinkling coming from amongst the trees. As we scanned the Sitka spruce boughs, our eyes fell on three dream catchers hanging from several branches. They had been tied off with monofilament fishing line. Each dream catcher had a small wind chime attached to it."

"Gruesome and unsettling thoughts flashed through my mind. All three of us looked at each other at about the same time. It was like we could smell the savagery all around us. One of my team members commented that his spine was tingling. The feeling was that deep."

"All three of us quickly diverted our eyes to the western horizon. We could see the silhouette of hand tools leaning up against several trees. On closer inspection, we found a spade shovel, a square point shovel, a pick-ax, and a pitchfork. We left all the tools in the location as we found them."

"It was at this point that our radio crackled, and we got summoned to link back up with the main body of our platoon." Katherine and Veronica seem terrified at my words. I am nauseated by the memory, so I stagger over toward the men's room.

Bewildered, beating, and bruised. Tongue lashed by the fiery serpent humiliated and ridiculed with incessant, malicious intent, devoured by his malignant distortion of reality on the edge of a forgotten land.

Chapter Eighteen:

Dirks Bakery at Ingra Street and 9th Avenue

Katherine can see that I am visibly distraught. Veronica is in the kitchen area getting me drinking water. *Do these ladies fully understand what we are involved with here? Is Veronica here as Maestro's eyes? Will they step back from me in fear as everyone else has in my life?*

"Katherine, I had Veronica put together the next segment of information for us. She has keen insight and skill for breaking down basic business models." We watch as Veronica opens her folder and shuffles out a small pile of paperwork onto the debrief table.

She has a strong voice. Her confidence is high as she begins her informal presentation for Katherine and me. "I am trying to use general table speak so that we can keep this simple. If you have any questions, please feel free to jump in at any time."

"Anthony, I am sure you think I am here to keep tabs on you. Yes, that is a part of my bigger assignment. I admit that is true. I'm your friend. I am Katherine's friend. If we all stay in our lanes and do our jobs, everything will work out. Are we all good?" she asks.

"Yes, I'm good so far," Katherine responds, nodding yes.

"I hope to feel good at some point," I retort. Veronica laughs while shaking her head as if she is in disbelief at my comment.

"Ok, here we go," Veronica says.

"Dirks Bakery was at the corner of Ingra Street and 9th Avenue here in Anchorage. Loosely translated, Ingra is a name that means a bullheaded woman with stubborn tendencies. I feel this fits the overall profile of most of Dirks victims, but it is not specific to all of his victims," Veronica's eyes focus intently on our faces.

"In the Occult and Bible, the number nine represents judgment, usually a final judgment. Was this accidental, incidental, or coincidental? Did Dirks knowingly choose this location because of the address? If he did not knowingly connect with the Ingra and 9th before he moved in, did he see it afterward?"

"I hate to, but we need to think like Dirks here for a moment. It hits him one day while he is standing in his window decorating a cake at Ingra Street and 9th Avenue. Does he start to feel invincible? He died, so we will never know the real answer," Veronica gives a perplexed sigh as she continues speaking.

"Now, let us take a closer peek at the environment Dirks was doing business in. It's 1981 in Anchorage, Alaska. Importing anything in bulk by air-cargo transportation was very expensive back then. A bakery is a margin business, meaning when all things are said, they who get their supplies by incurring the least financial expense wins the food game."

"Dirks was running a bakery. His hardware was heavy and bulky. Importing flour, sugar, and shortening in bulk is heavy and expensive as well. The food industry struggled to survive under these circumstances. Now, where does this all take us?"

"How does a man like this support a family of four? He owned a nice airplane. He was able to send his family on many vacations, sometimes for several months at a time. He had educational expenses for his children. He adorned his home with expensive wildlife mounts. His wife did work, but she claims they never mingled their funds."

"It just wasn't adding up. The more we looked, the more we realized that he was into something deeper, more sinister than it first appeared. The time he spent stalking and killing his victims consumed a large amount of time, which took his time away from his business. Who was helping him run the bakery in his absence? Was that person covering up for Dirks? Could they have been a co-conspirator?"

CHAPTER NINETEEN:

FORTY MILES OF EGO IN A PIPER SUPER CUB

"Why would Damon Dirks limit himself to forty miles in an airplane?" I ask Katherine and Veronica. "Any ideas on this? I mean, he could fly anywhere, right? Was it convenience? Was he trying to limit his fuel costs?"

"We also need to look at the location of most of his known gravesites. None of them are far from buildings, roads, bridges, and powerlines. This would increase the possibility of detection. Was he hoping to get caught? Was he that careless?"

"He seems always to have had some small glimpse of civilization available to him while he performed his dirty deeds. Was the big bad wolf afraid of the dark? Did his need to control his victims come from that same fear of the wilderness?"

"Maybe all of my thoughts are speculative. If either of you ladies has further insight, please share it at this time." *I feel bruised and battered, beaten down. My insides are churning again like a cocktail blender running at high speed. When will all this end?*

Katherine speaks up for the first time, "Anthony. Veronica. I am thinking we run with the general idea that he was afraid of the wilderness. His convenience was a priority. His hunting grounds were small. He stayed tight to his bakery and home at Old Harbor Avenue. He had so much activity going on in his life I am thinking avoiding any time crunch was an important element of his thought process."

Veronica responds, "Ok, I am following you, Katherine; I agree. If he would only fly forty miles to flirt on the edges of the wilderness, his drives would have tended to be shorter in their distance." Everyone is nodding yes. Silence envelopes the dimly lit room.

Veronica continues, "We know he confessed to bringing some of his victims to Old Harbor Avenue, where he engaged in his shameful acts. We can conclude he never brought any of his victims to his bakery. We also know he wasn't doing this act in his truck or car."

Veronica looks over at me, "Anthony, do you want to take it from here now?"

"Yes, Veronica. Thank you. I looked at one of his closest known burial sites, north of Fort Richardson near the Anchorage landfill area, where he accessed by road. This is approximately eight miles from his home by road. My mind was pondering all the missing victims, wondering if he had a central burial location, an established graveyard that he was using."

"So I took that eight-mile distance and reasoned that if he was looking for convenience, he might have found it somewhere closer to his home. The driving distance from his home to his bakery was a little over four miles. The distance from his home to the corner of W 4th Avenue and Denali Street, where he did most of his street prowling, is approximately five and a half miles. Both drives are less than six miles."

"Using a map, I located two areas both less than six miles from his home that would have provided him everything he needed—ease of access and a secluded area for privacy. The first location is in Far North Bicentennial Park off of Cambell Airstrip Road. The second location is No Man's Land located behind Doyon utility power plant, over on Arctic Valley Road."

CHAPTER TWENTY:

BLUE LIGHTS AND A HOWLING WOLF

It's been a cacophony of high-pitched piercing cries, chaotic, tumultuous, calling to me from their graves. Why didn't I fight more? Why didn't I go further? It makes you wonder, you know. Could we have stopped him sooner? Maybe if someone had given a little more care?

The PRC-77 field radio is crackling in my ear, and I am carrying an M-60 machine gun, affectionately known as the pig. I am locked and loaded with a 1,000 round belt of 7.62 mm ammunition. It's a sequence that gets played over and over up in Arctic Valley lately for my squad.

"De Luciano, move us out," hisses Sergeant Bell. "Let's rock, gentlemen," he whispers to the rest of my squad. "I want you guys moving slowly up the center of the road, maintain your distance integrity at all times. Let's rock." The 1st squad of the second platoon slowly crawls out from among the devil's club thriving on the high bank that lines Arctic Valley Road. We have strict orders to keep our eyes focused on the utility powerline trail down below us as we ascend the rugged mountain road. It is now 2000 hours.

Subtle hues of dying alpenglow guide us upward in our patrol. The Summit Nike launch site is our rally point. We have seven miles of harsh gravel road to traverse in fourteen hours. It is going to be a long night for us. Twenty miles round trip to return home to building #664.

About twenty minutes into our patrol, we get halted, "Halt! Get down and observe the utility plant," whispers Sergeant Bell. "I just saw blue lights flashing. There may be a police cruiser down there."

When I turn around, I don't see blue lights flashing, but I watch a vehicle flash its headlights three times. Everyone watches in complete silence. Sergeant Tenakanova is looking through his lowlight optic enhancer. We see the flash of the headlights again, three times.

The vehicles are pulled nose to nose next to the transformer station at the utility plant's powerline trail parking area. It looks like a police cruiser and a decent-looking pickup truck. They have their headlights on, and we can see silhouettes standing in between the vehicles. We watch as three shadows shimmer in the light below us.

Sergeant Bell huddles us up, "Listen, the police are here. We have no reason to stay tight and observe. Let's move out. No lights. No noise. Let's do this," he orders us.

Specialist Ackerman lifts his fist and rallies us to him, "You heard the Sarge lets rock this town tonight gentlemen, move out." His eyes are sparkling, revealing his love for this stuff. Patrols and long-range reconnaissance are his game.

It is now 2350 hrs. We can see the frightening glow from a blazing inferno burning down on the powerline trail. We are listening to a woman screaming, "I hate you! Stop hurting me. Why are you doing this to me? Don't kill me, I have kids! Don't kill me," her screaming continues.

Sergeant Bell gets on the radio. He is pleading with our operations command staff to direct law enforcement over to the utility power plant. He is describing what we are seeing and hearing. Every soldier in the squad hears the order that comes back over the radio, "1st squad stand down. Law enforcement is not our concern right now. You will move out and complete the mission."

It looks like the blazing inferno is going to ignite the surrounding forest. A twisting tail of sparks is swirling madly into the sky above the fire pit. We hear the woman scream one last time, "NO DON'T!" The sound of growling like a mad dog echoes up the ridgeline toward us. We are all asking Sergeant Bell if we should run back down. He shakes his head no.

Suddenly, a wolf starts howling down next to the fire. Irreverent, ominous, and chilling feelings flood over me as Sergeant Tenakanova looks back at us. "You guys are never going to believe this," he is saying. The lowlight optic enhancers are clenched tightly in his trembling hand.

"There is a white male ritualistically dancing naked around the fire pit with nothing but his boots and glasses on. I am not seeing anyone else alive in the camp," he sullenly says.

CHAPTER TWENTY-ONE:

MOOSE RUN GOLF COURSE ANCHORAGE ALASKA

"What are the cops doing up here again?" asks PFC Nelson. "AST has jurisdiction up here, not the local Anchorage Police Department," he explains to us.

As the police cruiser slowly creeps toward us winding its way down chilly Arctic Valley Road, our platoon spreads open like the red sea parting for Moses. We break into two small columns, one column moves to the left of the road, the other column shifts to the right, and we allow the police cruiser to drive up the middle. I notice it has number sixty-three stenciled on the side of the car near the back door. It is now 0445 hrs.

The person driving is a very young police officer, heavyset with thick, black, curly hair. I notice his uniform is disheveled. The officer never engages us. He keeps his eyes straight forward, never glancing to his right or his left.

One of our noncommissioned officers asks us all a question, "Did you feel the fear coming from that car, gentlemen?"

"He never even looked at us, Sarge." PFC Bryan replies.

"Sergeant Tenekanova, should we make contact with the MP's?" Specialist Rabitoy asks.

"No. Move out in a single file line, gentlemen. Take control of the middle of the road. Let's rock," Sergeant Tenekanova orders us.

We walk silently through the golf course area. It's slightly chilly but surprisingly no wind. As we pass by the Doyon utility power plant, Specialist Rabitoy rallies us into the little parking area on the left-hand side of the road. We take breaks in here a lot next to the transformer cage. It is three miles from the front gate of Fort Richardson, which is the perfect distance to stop and take a break when you are two hours into a long-range patrol.

"Smoke 'em if you got 'em," Specialist Eine shouts out. Ironically, Eine doesn't smoke.

A lone man is standing at the rear of a pickup truck parked just past the transformer cage. One of our noncommissioned officers barks out an order, "De Luciano, pull rear guard for us while we make contact with this civilian over here."

I break off from the group and move toward the pickup truck, watching as my two noncommissioned officers hail the individual. "Excuse us, we need to ask you a few questions this morning if that is okay with you, sir?" one of them calmly asks.

"Ah, s-s-sure. If there is any way I can be of help, please let me know," I hear the man respond. He continues, "I see you guys in this here area, is there anything going on? Maybe I could help if there was something you need help with?"

One of the noncommissioned officers responds, "We do need your help this morning, sir. We need to see your identification. We also need you to take your rifle off your shoulder and give control of the weapon to Sergeant Schlick over here. Can you do that for us?"

With his eyes cast down and nervously shuffling his feet, the man complies with the request. One of the noncommissioned officers is inspecting the identification card. I hear him ask, "Mr. Dirks, what are you doing out here this early?" Before Dirks can respond, the noncommissioned officer continues, "We are about to launch a three-week live-fire training exercise, sir. It is going to be extremely dangerous."

Mr. Dirks replies, "I told you guys before when we met, I am glassing for sheep up in here. I told you about this the last time we spoke, Sergeant. Can I be of any help here today?"

"If you venture up the road, be warned you may get yourself killed. We can't stop you from being up here unless we launch a real alert. You're probably safe down in the powerline. The United States Government wouldn't want to be responsible for destroying infrastructure, but we still have to give you a stern warning to be very careful up in here."

Mr. Dirks is nodding his tilted head while he listens, "No p-p-problem guys. Let me get out while I can. Be sure

I am thankful for what you have just told me, Sergeant. You can be s-s-sure I am."

The second platoon allows Mr. Dirks to proceed and drive away around the bend, and over the hill, we watch him descend. He never flinched. His nerves of steel held steady, coiled like a spring and ready to pounce. Casual, calm, having a good walk out here today, can't you see.

Scorched earth among the coals, all of them now rest upon the permafrost, deep within overturned soil, quaking trees adorned with a tinkling talisman, his waiting, and worn shovel leans against a withered tree.

CHAPTER TWENTY-TWO:

DREAM CATCHERS, WIND CHIMES, AND NOW SPIDERS

I can see the glow of the perimeter light through blizzard-like conditions. Unsettling thoughts drift in my mind. Scathed by sharp disapproval, their frozen hearts stopped in time.

Katherine is hugging me tightly, "Anthony, I am so proud of you. Your tenacity is admirable. You are relentless. I love you so much," she whispers into my ear.

Veronica steps from the lady's restroom a little disheveled and wild-eyed. "I need a food break. Anyone for ordering take-out? I can call in some Thai food if that will work for everyone?" she asks. Both of us nod yes.

Katherine responds, "I want dumplings and spring-rolls please, no sauces. See if they can send some black tea."

"Please order me dumplings and chicken satay. The tea sounds like a great idea," I respond.

"Sweet, that's easy enough," Veronica casually announces as she moves over toward the phone. We watch as she reads the menu before picking up the phone to call in the order.

When Veronica rejoins us, Katherine takes over the conversation. "The purpose of a dream catcher is to catch dreams. That is, to trap bad or evil dreams and channel good dreams to the sleeper," she continues.

"Essentially, a dream catcher is intended to manipulate the spirit world. Why would Dirks use these talismans? Was he showing an eternal concern for his victims?" she asks.

Bewildered, I exclaim, "Listen, we may never know his actual intent ladies, our concern is any curses he may have cast over the graveyard. How do we navigate through what appears to be a web of deception? Did he cast a curse of resistance? Why has this fallen on so many closed ears over the years? My military unit reported everything we saw to our chain of command."

Veronica and Katherine watch me with a look of admiration, maybe even intrigue. It causes me to feel uncomfortable. My stomach starts doing flips because I do not like being in the spotlight. *Why has this fallen on me? Has the universe cursed me? Can I sense a light at the end of all this?*

"Ladies, I want us to consider the wind chimes that Dirks would hang in the trees. Over the years, it has always been assumed that a wild animal would partially uncover some remains that may be stumbled upon by a hunter someday. They hoped this would help law enforcement discover the graveyard."

"Metal wind chimes create a metallic tinkling. All animals are wary of metal sounds. Hunters try to avoid making any metallic clicks if possible when in the field. Dirks was using that cautionary instinct to keep the predators away. To illustrate firsthand, let me tell you a story about what we observed."

"My platoon had been deployed for fourteen days deep up inside Arctic Valley. Most of our maneuvers took place around Temptation Peak and in the surrounding valleys. On day thirteen orders came through, we were standing down and shifted into extraction mode."

"We found a shortcut, a trail that brought us over to Arctic Valley Road just below the ski lodge. When we got to the main road, we took control of the middle and started our descent. A constant wind was blowing up the mountain directly into our faces."

"When we came to the city view turnout Sergeant Foche raised his fist to halt us. He was pointing down toward the Doyon utility powerline trail. Everyone saw the big black spot highlighted against intense greenery and the beige sand of the powerline trail. We were looking at a large black bear."

Exasperated, I continue, "Or so it seemed. It became apparent that the bear's fur was standing up on end. It was facing west and staring intently at the treeline across the trail. It started huffing and stomping its two front paws against the ground for about fifteen seconds. The bear then turned to its left and started running away from the powerline."

"We watched and listened as the bear crashed through the brush, shrubs, and small trees. It stumbled across Arctic Valley Road and continued running over the ridge. We saw the bear look back several times over its shoulder while running. You could see what appeared to be intense fear in its eyes."

Completely out of breath after speaking, I notice Katherine is slipping her right shoe off her foot. She is peering intently toward a corner over near the photocopier with predation in her eyes. Veronica and I watch her stalk slowly across the floor with her shoe raised above her head.

Bam! Her arm swings with deadly precision. She is skilled. Red cheeks betray her excitement. Smiling with glee, she wildly exclaims, "Got him. Spiders tend to creep me out."

Chapter Twenty-Three

CIA Profiles De Luciano's Mafia Lineage

Veronica seems perplexed by something. "Anthony, I am missing something here? You have never been clear on why you were selected? I mean, how did the chain of command choose you for this mission?" Katherine is nodding in agreement with her question.

Slightly hesitant, I respond, "Ok, this gets a little complex and multilayered. Some of what I am about to tell you was a surprise to myself. It happened back on Fort Leonard Wood, Missouri in February of 1981." Katherine and Veronica sit up. They both lean forward, listening intently to my words.

"I was on a twenty-four-hour guard duty cycle with Private Freeman. We had been assigned to patrol an area of the base that housed many military history and artifacts. It was considered to be a hot zone, meaning all eyes needed to stay vigilant."

"All of the walking paths in the area converge at an intersection, and there is an old church located here. While patrolling along the intersection area at about 0130 hours, we saw three black vans pull into the church parking area. We watched as they turned, and all of them backed up toward the front entrance of the church."

Katherine raises her hand, "Anthony do you have live ammunition while out on guard duty during basic training?" she asks.

"Yes. Three rounds each. No rounds loaded in the chamber," I reply.

I continue, "Private Freeman and I cautiously moved toward the vans. Without warning, we got blinded by a spotlight from one of the vehicles beaming directly at our faces. A loud voice was yelling for us to drop our weapons and get down on the ground. We did not comply. We stood our ground."

Hysterical laughter started coming from the shadows, and a voice called out, "Privates, I am Colonel Jantz, be at ease." We watch a solitary figure moving toward us. I can see a sidearm strapped on his hip.

A bearded man emerges from the shadow smiling with his hand extended. We both snap to attention and salute him. He responds, "At ease, trainees. I told you both to stand down. Now follow me. We need your help unloading these vehicles," Freeman and I exchange worried looks.

Private Freeman speaks up, "Sir, we need to request an identification check. Place your ID on the ground for me, and take three steps backward," he commands the Colonel. Colonel Jantz shakes his head in disgust.

"Trainee, you are on some dangerous ground right now. Stand down and follow me," he snarls.

We follow him over to the three vans. The back doors are open, and we can see they are loaded full of assorted gun cases and ammunition containers. One of the other officers engages Colonel Jantz, "Colonel will these two trainees need a higher security clearance?"

The Colonel succinctly responds, "They received clearance two days ago, Captain." Turning to Freeman and myself, Colonel Jantz barks out, "Unload these vans with my guys. I will meet you both inside. You can never tell anyone what we are about to show you. Understood?" he demands.

Fearfully I start nodding yes. Quizzically, Freeman and I look at each other while shaking our heads. We sullenly begin the unload. I am mesmerized by the silence as we work.

Counting Freeman and myself, there are twelve men. Three drivers, with two escorts per vehicle, plus Colonel Jantz. The escort team is wearing masks and armed with Mossberg's twelve-gauge shotguns. The drivers have their faces painted in beige-grey camouflage with green bandanas wrapped around their heads. Only the Colonel is clean-faced above his beard, and he is unmasked.

Upon entering the building, I see an elegant tapestry. Tassels dangle from almost every curtain. Grotesque statues surrounded by stained glass become a silent witness to our arbitrary, unrestrained ideology, weapons in a church.

Colonel Jantz stops walking, spins around, and looks each of us in our eyes, "Gentleman, what I am about to show you will need to be kept as a secret. This building is a secret. Follow me."

We walk through the sanctuary area and go up behind the pulpit into a back room. Jantz walks over to the wall and flips a switch. We hear a dim humming sound like an electric motor. He smiles and nods toward a hole opening up in the middle of the floor. Freeman and I are wide-eyed. I can feel sweat beading up on my forehead in anticipation.

"Gentleman, all cargo goes down these stairs, please," Jantz commands. We descend into a ballroom adorned with some unusual violet-lavender tapestry. Along each wall are hundreds of glass cases filled with weapons. Each section of the room houses weapons from different eras of USA warfare back to the Revolutionary War with the British in the 1770s.

Once the work is complete, Colonel Jantz barks out, "De Luciano, follow me. Freeman, you go back outside and commence on your guard duty rounds alone. Private De Luciano will link up with you when I am done with him here." Freeman snaps to attention, "Yes, sir."

As Private Freeman leaves, I follow Jantz into a small cubicle area surrounded by acoustic waffle panels. He has me take a seat while curtly stating, "Sit here, De Luciano."

Jantz starts talking, "I am going to jump right into this, De Luciano. We want you to function as eyes and ears for the United States Government," I am bewildered by his words.

"Your armed services vocational aptitude battery, or ASVAB test results are spectacular. I would kill to have scores like those, De Luciano. I understand you will be operating in the Pacific theater after basic training. Is this correct, Private?"

"Yes, sir," I respond. He leans across the table. He has coal-black eyes that radiate an intensity I have never experienced. "I want to talk with you about your family history De Luciano."

He catches me off guard, "Huh? My family? Are you out of your mind, Colonel?" he starts laughing.

"De Luciano, I have been told that I am out of my mind by many people. Yes, I am an insane soldier. Thank you for asking me and showing your concern. Now listen up, kid."

"When we accessed the world locator to trace your heritage, we found a curious connection to Charles Lucania's younger sister, Concetta Lucania. They originated from Palermo, Sicilia, Italy." He has my absolute attention for sure.

I respond, "My great-grandmother Francesca De Luciano was from Palermo, Sicilia?" Jantz is smiling, nodding vigorously.

"I love your locution De Luciano. Yes, she was. Concetta and Francesca may very well be first cousins, meaning you are Mafia royalty," my head snaps up.

"Me Mafia royalty? Are you crazy? What are you saying, Colonel?" his eyes sparkle like black diamonds at my question.

"When you get to Alaska, we would like you to accept an assignment. Can you do that for us?" he's intent as he continues. "Listen to the words coming out of my mouth Anthony. I am your friend right now. The guys on the other end in Alaska will not be. Understood?" I am nodding yes, but I have no idea what he means.

"I need you to define this operation for me, Colonel. It seems unclear," I reply.

"After you arrive in Alaska, there will come a day when you get escorted into your commanding officer's private chambers. You are going to be introduced to two CID officers. They are not your friends. No matter what you do, you must act surprised, like you have no idea what is happening to you. Do you understand me?" he demands.

"Yes, sir," I acknowledge.

"We are embedding you into an organized crime faction that we suspect is running an international human trafficking enterprise. This is serious and deadly business, De Luciano. If not done properly, you will be dead. No turning back."

Katherine and Veronica seem bedazzled. I need to relax. I usually wouldn't turn to alcohol, but this is different.

Looking toward the front door, I ask the ladies, "Do either of you two ladies want to get out of here and go for a drink?" They both nod yes without hesitating. Veronica speaks up.

"Any thoughts on where we are going?" she asks.

I respond, "Yes. Carpentier's Cocktail over at 335 Boniface Parkway. Call us a taxi, please, and you all get ready to rock this town tonight." Both ladies squirm with unbridled enthusiasm.

While I stand staring into the setting sun, a mirage appears to be shimmering on the horizon. I can see a titillating woman covered in gold. As the seductress rises from the ash, melodious chimes resonate across our land before her.

CHAPTER TWENTY-FOUR:

NIKE SUMMIT LAUNCH SITE ARCTIC VALLEY, ALASKA

"Sergeant check this out? We have a Piper Super Cub breaking north into our airspace. Have we locked the airspace down yet? Do I need to record the tail number, Sergeant?" I ask.

Sergeant Essman walks over to my fighting position and hands me his notepad to record the tail number. "Hey, Sarge, take a look at this. It's a little terrifying. A girl is crying and pounding on the window while the pilot is trying to pull her back. It looks like they may be struggling."

Both of us take turns glassing the plane with a high-powered sniper scope mounted on my M60 machine-gun. We have a clear view as it floats past us below the ridge we are on. The woman continues frantically pounding on the window. We can see she has reddish-blonde hair and her mascara stained across her face.

Sergeant Tenekanova speaks up, "Somethings wrong with this picture, gentlemen. Keep your eyes on that plane.

Let's see if we can spot where the pilot lands." All eyes of the 1st squad follow the blue and white Piper Super Cub as it flies. Unfortunately, the sun is bright and blinds the plane to our view in the morning haze.

Sergeant Tenekanova looks at me, "Did you get that tail number De Luciano? Please tell me yes, soldier?" he pleads.

Disheartened, I am shaking my head no, "I was only able to record the first letter and the last three characters Sergeant, I have N--8--9--Z." Sergeant Tenekanova confirms the numbering sequence with me while making a notation in his field journal.

"I am recording N--8--9--Z. Is this correct, PFC De Luciano?" he asks.

"Yes, Sergeant, that is correct," I reply. I feel dejected for not being able to see and record the complete tail number. Have you ever felt like a total failure? For some reason, right now, I have that feeling surging through me.

Wanting to be alone, I turn and stare north toward Mount Denali. I know she is there because Mount Foraker is visible right next door to her. Alpenglow encrusted peaks glow above the clouds, like a beacon, taunting at my heart. My head swivels to grab a glimpse of Mount Susitna to my south, and I see her silhouette writhing on the horizon, long lost in a chaotic dance.

With the rising sun blinding me, I can see her silhouetted, balanced, and poised on the pinnacle of a sprawling pyramid. When the woman looks over toward me, I can see blotches of red covering her face, and tears are dripping off of her nose.

Chapter Twenty-Five:

Prowling the Edges of Insanity

Veronica Sage is on a roll this morning. Katherine is cuddled up next to her on the couch.

"How does a family man engage in so many murders? A businessman? Big game hunter? These are all time-consuming lifestyles. Combine the three, and it becomes a huge time crunch on anybody brave enough to take it all on."

"Now throw prolific serial killer into the mix. Say what? Who has this much time available? All this hustle and bustle makes me feel exhilarated just thinking about it," she declares.

Katherine speaks up, "Let's not forget kidnapper? That seems to be his biggest thrill to me. It's the one thing all his victims have in common—the heist, his stalk, then the takedown. We must remember that he did not kill all of his kidnap victims. Many were for-profit, filthy lucre as some have called it."

"We need to step back and take a deeper look," Veronica replies. "What is the one common denominator in all of his crimes against women besides the kidnapping? Fear! It's fear," she shouts out. "I am seeing Damon Dirks thriving on fear."

"Ladies, I agree with every one of these angles. Think of what we were saying earlier about most of his known gravesites? They are all close to and within view of man-made structures," I remind them.

"Now, one thought I have about this is that he left them next to waymarks that would be visible from the air. Allowing him to look down upon his victims over and over again every time he flew his plane north. Reliving the memories in his mind over and over while he flew. He would have most likely felt like he was above them again, making them lower than himself."

"Ok, I am following you, Anthony," Veronica responds. "So we have him up there flying, looking down, either, to his left, or his right upon his scattered trophies, he feels a big thrill. In his mind, he is a real big boy up there."

"Yes," I reply. "But when the plane is on the ground again, fear sets in. He has more fear when he is on the ground. What is one thing every sentient being looks for when they become afraid?" I ask.

Katherine smiles, "A protector," she says.

"Yes. Someone that can coddle them. Make them feel safe. This brings us full circle back to Veronica's theory of an enabler or co-conspirator. Who was protecting Damon Dirks?" I muse.

"Law enforcement has long suspected if he had a co-conspirator, they came from the military or the ranks of law enforcement itself. Maybe it was closer to home," I continue. "Let's imagine Dirks hunting and killing with one of his employees for once," the ladies are intrigued, eagerly following my every word.

"My platoon was seeing an Anchorage Police Department cruiser, number sixty-three in Arctic Valley regularly. APD did not and still does not have jurisdiction up there. The ASTs own that jurisdiction to this day."

Katherine and Veronica exchange a curious glance as I continue speaking, "Back in the day we are talking about, there were a lot of older police cruisers for sale in Anchorage. Dirks may have purchased one to use as a decoy, allowing him or his co-conspirator to not only approach women without detection, but also after the kidnapping, they would feel comfortable transporting them around town."

"I mean, dwell about it with me for a moment. It's a normal occurrence to see the police transporting unruly prisoners in their back seat. It is also normal to see prisoners secured with handcuffs. In Anchorage back in the day, the police picked up a lot of street workers, most of them were young women."

"They would have blended right into the landscape," Veronica exclaims.

"Exactly," I respond. "Nothing to see here folks move along."

CHAPTER TWENTY-SIX:

WHO DID THAT MONSTER TAKE FROM US

A child's laughter. Your sister's embrace. An aunt's surprise visit. Until death before we part. Lost generations of love and laughter have disappeared because of him.

All of the women possessed a shadowy innocence hindered by foggy despair, aspirations of grandeur crushed by clapping thunder over the tundra. A wolf's howl had led them astray until they found themselves dancing with the devil himself. He demanded of them that their show must go on.

My name is Sue. I arrived in Alaska looking for that one big chance now I am overcome with a nagging dread that something dire is about to happen to me. I am feeling isolated with no one to confide in. A frozen emptiness has taking up residence in my chest and is working its way up my windpipes, trying to choke me with massive concern.

Pristine wilderness is nowhere around me. The skyline darkened by chain-link fences cluttered with clinging newspapers. Gritty-sounding exhaust pipes with jagged edges spew pungent clouds of toxic fumes toward my hardened face as I struggle to walk against the withering winds. I become choked by the trailing dust through a cloud-filled, endless day and amid dark, sleepless nights.

Taxi horns constantly blaring, the hiss of screeching air-brakes pumping, the traffic continues to taunt me. Discarded liquor bottles reflecting small flashes of light in the sun adorn the gutter. Busted, broken lives are strewn across the curb before me as I wander along W 4th Avenue in downtown Anchorage, Alaska. I can sense my future lies ahead of me just around the next corner.

What is wrong with me? I want that pretty dress in the storefront window, but I have no money. Who am I to think that I deserve this dress? I am a person that doesn't win the reward. Maybe tomorrow will be different. Quit punishing yourself, Sue.

When I was growing up, people went out of their way to make me feel uncomfortable. Their daily jeers of depravity clouding my mind, "Hey, ugly dog. Skank ho. Lose some weight. Nobody will ever love you. Fatso. Did your mother have any kids that lived?"

Is this living? Can people see me? Why did I come north to Alaska? Every time I pull on my cold, soggy gloves, one has to wonder about all this, you know. Could I have done more with my life? Why do I feel so empty and hollow like a fluttering leaf?

I'm just a woman struggling to get ahead on the mean streets of Anchorage. I keep coming across bad manners, inappropriate and disturbing behavior. I heard a rumor about a man walking around with filthy clothes and dark rotten teeth that kills street girls. They say he can radiate evil with his hard, black eyes.

A car horn beeping draws my attention. I stop walking and turn toward the sound to look. A hoarse and harsh-sounding voice shouts out from the open window, "You're a no-good whore. Why don't you go home where you came from."

CHAPTER TWENTY-SEVEN:

HUSH NOW MY BABY

When you look through a crowd, who do you see? Is it your reflection or their lost stares looking back at you? With a darting glance, you search among the shadows while eagerly awaiting one last hug. Is that her knocking on my door? Please come home tonight, stay safe. I need you here with me, my love.

Oh, wretched woman that I have become. Grief-stricken, my heart is crushed beyond repair. That animal performed despicable acts against my daughter's humanity. He degraded her as if she were nothing. Her soul has been seemingly vanquished, stomped by an insidious aberration of cowardness.

The very depths of hell became personified and amplified through Damon Dirks. He was polished and lifted to behold for public adoration. Richly fulfilled by family rewards and enhanced by spousal privilege, his life was allowed to go on. Did he have no shame?

What was he thinking on a Thursday night? Was this his version of wilderness recreation? He destroyed human life with handcuffs, pillowcases, and chains. A roaring fire, crackling with white-hot embers, stomping and howling into the moonless night like a savage beast.

Hush, mom is silently cowering in her home while waiting for you tonight. Come in, sit down and fall tenderly into my loving arms one last time. Let me embrace your inner child while my moist lips linger on your forehead. Please, God, let this moment last forever.

Thrilled by their shouts of terror, did he willingly mock them back in glee? With his taunting shrieks and grimy hands beating them, busting and breaking them down, their street-fighting spirits lingered. My daughter, Sue, unwillingly stood on the jagged edge of Satan's dark abyss while being forced to look down. *Did she look up and cry out for me? What did she see just before she died? Was I in her final thoughts?*

CHAPTER TWENTY-EIGHT:

WHY DIDN'T MY MOTHER COME HOME

"*N*o, I have kids. Don't kill me! I hate you!" *Suddenly silenced by the devil's claw while writhing in anguish on the forest floor.*

Everyone keeps telling me my mother is never coming home to see me. Some people tell me she never had any love for me. Now with all these conflicting thoughts, I can barely remember her smiling face.

I need to know what happened? Was it that guy Damon Dirks? Why did he have to kill all those girls? Where did he bury my mother? Did my mother die because of me?

Can you see the northern lights? It's snowing outside now. I don't want you looking into my soul. Blanketed by frozen dread, I wander from tavern to tavern along W 4th Avenue in Anchorage, Alaska. While stumbling through one last creaky door for the night, my body seems to dance with the late-night breeze as I attempt to gather my fragmented thoughts.

Amidst the warming glow of neon light flashing from within the confines of the drinking den I just vacated, I find myself surrounded by several street women of the night. They are all curvaceous, young women. *Was this my mother's world?*

"Hey cutie, are you looking for a date? Who do we have here? You going out tonight, honey? Hey, lover boy, share some of that sugar over here with me. One hundred dollars will get you all of this and a whole lot more. What can mommy do for her baby tonight?"

I find myself surrounded by six lecherous ladies. All of them have blonde hair. Their sexual desires seem offensive and perverse to me. *Is this how the world saw my mother? Is this the perception that the community has of these women?* For my sanity, I need to cleanse these thoughts from my mind.

Music trickling from the shadows calls to me from the great beyond. An empty whiskey bottle gets launched at me from an open window of a passing car. Before I can jump out of the projectile's way, smashing glass attempts to shred my ankles. Fortunately, my high leather boots and wool socks protect me from being cut.

Honk-honk, the brassy note of a car horn interrupts me. I look down at a decent-looking sedan. There is a cute girl, short red hair, ruddy complexion speaking with me through the open window, "Hey cutie, do you need a ride?"

Wow, she seems like a nice girl. Maybe my luck is about to change for the better, "Why would I let you drive me home tonight?" I ask her.

The smiling girl brings her car to a stop. I lean against the roof of her car and ask her again, "Why am I letting you do this? Have we met before? Do you know me?"

"Honey, Henrietta knows everybody, jump in, stop wasting time," she teases.

Coyly, I respond, "Go ahead, Henrietta, then tell me my name, go for it, guess my name."

"Joshua?" she seems to be half asking.

"Close, but no. It's Nick. So you don't know me, and you didn't know my name. Am I still allowed to get in your car for that ride home? I ask.

Prodding me while staring straight ahead through her windshield, she warns me, "Beware, if you get in my car, I am a monster. Ggrrhh, she growls. Seriously though, if you get in, things may go a little differently for you tonight. Are you sure you're going to be okay with that, Nick?"

I have a good feeling about this one. I like where it's going, so I respond, "Let's tear this town up, get me away from here, Henrietta," while quickly getting into her car.

Before I turn around, I feel a thudding slam against the side of my face. My left ear is ringing loudly. It feels like I got punched by a heavyweight boxer. My left hand goes up to protect my face. I struggle with Henrietta to keep her from grabbing and twisting my arm violently down toward the center console of her car.

Throbbing pain shoots along my wrist as she wrestles a pair of handcuffs onto me. I hear the loud metallic snap as they tighten. She leans toward me, grimacing in my face, "Sucker, I got you, little boy. You need to learn a lesson, and I am going to teach it to you. I am the black widow of these streets, and it's my job to punish bad boys."

Bad boys? This girl is insane. Thrashing against the handcuffs to get free, I start screaming, "Let me go!" She slams me again with her icy revolver.

"Shut up over there. Do as I tell you, and everything will go good for you."

Can you believe this guy? Did he think I was that easy? What would Detective Hildebrandt think of me now? I love to control men. They are not allowed to have control over me.

Chapter Twenty-Nine:

A Mystery Lady Meets with Yohann Ru'desh

How long have I been sitting in this dreary place waiting for a dream? I need a man so I can wrap my legs around him while keeping my tips held high, start reeling in nice and slow. Gaze into my eyes. Who do you see? Can you sense me? Have I been obliterated yet?

This neighborhood of ours, this town we all live in, offers us grit for the taking. Are there any real men left in Alaska? They all seem to be swimming through a murky alphabet soup. APD, AST, ATF, CIA, CID, DEA, FBI. Are there any genuine cowboys left alive? One has to wonder, you know.

KGB agent Yohann Ru'desh has proven himself different. He possesses a clarity of mind, which helps him maintain singleness of purpose. His strong hands accentuate a muscular frame and short-cropped black hair with a chiseled chin.

He creates a yearning inside of me, like a fluttering. I can freely do things with him I have never dreamed of doing with my husband, Damon. I become like a brazen witch and a no-good whore when I am with Yohann. He makes me feel dirty, and I love it.

People do not understand how inappropriate and disturbing my husband Damon is. I need to escape his savagery. This assignment has gone on for me long enough. I feel we need to cut our ties and move on from here. *Why did I accept this assignment? I was young. How could I have known? Me KGB?*

Yohann has just entered through the shadowy doorway. It causes me to take a grateful swallow that he is here for me. Looking concerned and slightly agitated, he approaches me from across the bar area. My stomach rolls into a flip, and I struggle to maintain my composure.

With a low voice, Yohann says, "Dahla, my lover, you're here? I panicked that you wouldn't accept the invitation. I can see my fear was unfounded. I love you more than anything in this world. Thank you very much for coming. I am so grateful."

"Yohann, take me to Moscow right now. I want to leave the United States as quickly as possible."

His eyes widen while he holds his hand out to me, "What happened? Are you all right? Did he hurt you again, that dirty crook? Let me order you a white Russian. Bartender two frozen white Russians, please, at your convenience."

Dahla seems scared to me, depressed, maybe even suicidal now that I take a good look at her. *What have I put her through? When she learns the truth, will she be able to forgive me? How could I have been so cruel all these years?* I can't let her connect me to the Maestro, not yet.

"Yohann, I feel sick like my insides are curling, and it makes me want to peel my skin off. The cymbals are gone, but my head is still pounding from all the lies we have told. My life is a big lie. I don't believe in God, I don't love my husband, and I never wanted to have children. I am lost."

I reach my hand out to her, keeping my voice low, "My home in Moscow will provide shelter from pursuit, danger, or trouble for you," I assure Dahla. "First, you will need to liquidate all your physical assets in the United States. I can help you with that task."

CHAPTER THIRTY:

THE KNIK RIVER'S SILTY GRAVE

My taxi cab driver is peering intently into her rearview mirror when she announces, "ASTs are following behind us, I'm not sure, but they may have a warrant out for my arrest," she says with an undertone of derision.

We turn left onto Tudor Road from the Boniface Parkway. A black Range Rover sport utility vehicle pulls along our right side. I can see there are four passengers dressed in dark clothes. Now I am getting worried that they might be here for me.

I shout up to my driver, "Can you stop at a convenience store when we come to one? I just need to grab a bottle of water."

"Sure thing, cowboy. There is a Tesoro gas station about a mile up the road here. We will stop there," she says.

My driver puts her signal on and pulls us into the parking lot of the Tesoro gas station and convenience store. The police cruiser drives past us, but the Range

Rover follows us into the parking lot. I watch it pull up to the gas pumps for fuel.

"We can take five minutes here," my driver says.

"Thank you. Let me give you these twenty dollars now. It will cover the fare and tip. Hopefully, I will be right back," I respond. She throws me a dirty look as I exit her car.

"Will this bottle of water be it for you today, sir?" the cashier inquires.

"Yes, it will," I respond.

As I exit the store, I see two AST cruisers pulling into the parking lot. I turn toward shouting from the gas pump area, "Down, get down." Three men are running in my direction with their handguns pointing at me, "Get down on the ground now, or we will shoot you," they command.

I drop to my knees with my hands up, my bottle of water falls to the ground and rolls away from me, "Don't shoot, Don't shoot, I am unarmed, don't shoot me," I scream.

"We are federal agents. You are being detained for questioning Mr. De Luciano. Please allow us to search you. Do you have any weapons?" one of the agents asks me.

"I am unarmed. Don't shoot. I am going to lay face down, with my hands and feet spread out. You can search me, no problem," I respond.

After the body-search, two ASTs put me in body chains and lead me into one of their cruisers. A burly trooper leans in and whispers, "I seriously hate you."

The Range Rover pulled away from the gas pumps and drove over to the same area as the troopers. I can hear one of the federal agents explaining that they are taking me out to Fort Richardson for questioning and want me to follow them.

As we start driving, one of the officers shouts back, "You're looking at twenty-five to life, De Luciano; I hope they throw the key away on you. Leavenworth is going to be your final address," he sneers. Both men start laughing.

When we arrive in Fort Richardson, I get brought to a small conference room in a building that houses a signal company. They are in charge of communications for the base. I get introduced to a judge advocate general. He is a military officer who advises the government on court-martial and administers the conduct of court-martial.

One of the agents from the Range Rover is also present. He introduces himself to everyone in the room as Federal Bureau of Investigation's (FBI's) National Affairs agent Tom Hawk. Agent Hawk looks over at me with a look of contempt.

"De Luciano, you guaranteed Cold Case investigators that Damon Dirks buried Angie Altman's body in Arctic Valley. How could you possibly know this?"

"My name is Anthony De Luciano. I have done nothing wrong. It's always the right time to do the right thing. I supplied AST and FBI with many firsthand accounts of my interactions with Mr. Damon Dirks. My military unit was in a position to encounter and observe Mr. Dirks regularly in an area he frequented to glass for Dall sheep."

"This area has been affectionately known as No Man's Land for decades and is located in Arctic Valley bordered by a utility powerline trail. We engaged Dirks at the transformer cage numerous times. After multiple recons of the area, we determined there was a graveyard in the location."

"When police arrested Damon Dirks, I realized that all the screaming we heard up in Arctic Valley, and all the bonfires we observed, may have been associated with multiple homicides. I do realize it is speculative to finger Dirks. I can't wrap my head around the thought there may have been two killers on the loose in the same area, at the same time."

"I heard that Damon Dirks partially confessed he threw Angie Altman's dead body from the Knik River bridge. I need to assume he was referring to the Old Knik River bridge because the new bridge is out on the main highway, and it has a lot of traffic." There's no way he brought her in there from the time he kidnapped her on Wednesday, December 2 to Sunday, December 6. There were just too many people using both bridge locations during that time.

"Did he keep her hostage longer than five days? Possibly, but we may never know, so let me explain my thought process from what I saw back in the day," I reply.

"December 1981, operation Arctic Star was held at Fort Greely, Alaska. Black Rapids Glacier and Donnelly Dome both acted as center stage for different stages of the mission. Several airborne brigades from Fort Cambell, Kentucky, and Fort Bragg, North Carolina, traveled north to Alaska to participate."

"The entire 172nd Infantry Brigade from Alaska was involved. The 4/23rd Infantry Battalion acted as the vanguard during the mission. Elmendorf, AFB, and Fort Richardson went on full alert status, on Monday,

November 30. Troops from the lower forty-eight started arriving at Elmendorf on Tuesday, December 1."

"While a forward observation contingency of about three-hundred soldiers from the 172nd Infantry Brigade was airlifted north to Fort Greely, a high percentage of the arriving troops from the lower forty-eight convoyed north driving the Glenn Highway. The troop arrivals and convoy got spread out over six days until Sunday, December 6."

"We set up a triage area on the Old Glenn Highway in a pullout area just before the Old Knik River bridge, where S Old Glenn Highway meets with E Knik River Road. It was an area the arriving troops could divert to off the new Glenn Highway to seek medical attention, clothing items, and food. Because of the inclement weather in the vicinity of the bridge, we established a chokepoint for security."

"Each military vehicle that passed through the choke point got inspected for proper tires and chains. Safety was a concern. Every person down to the last soldier was encouraged to hydrate at all times. We set up a water point as a refill station in the same location as the triage tents. There was a lot of activity, twenty-four hours a day, for six to seven days."

"We also have to remember in December that the river is almost always frozen. If it's not, there are large ice flows that clog the river. Then we must mention the many islands situated about a mile and a half below the Old Knik River bridge that could act as collection spots for the body to get tangled on. The river tends to be shallow in that location, on average running three to twelve feet deep."

"Once you clear the islands, the river breaks up into a braided section of narrower muddy water that makes it even more unlikely the body washed out to the Knik Arm of Cook Inlet. Those are the reasons why I do not think he threw Angie Altman into the Knik River from the bridge."

"Please, remember, he could not fly her out. The airspace was closed down over the military bases."

CHAPTER THIRTY-ONE:

TONIGHT YOUR NAME IS INGRA

"Hey, boss, how are you doing today? What's going on outback? It looks like someone is doing work on the foundation. Do you need any assistance?" my employee Jason asks.

"No. S-s-stay away from that hole it's, deep. I am repairing some cracks. That's what is going on. I will get done s-s-soon, and the hole will be filled back in," I reply.

"Thank you, Jason, but I need you inside here doing production work and overseeing the end-of-the-day cleanup. I will be away for two days starting tomorrow. Will you be good running things for me?" I ask him.

"Sure thing, no problem, boss," he replies.

Detective Hildebrandt is smart. He will be watching my plane. I can't use my truck now because it is noticeable on the streets. I was able to convince my wife to take our children away for the summer so I can use her car. I can't let my recent arrest, law enforcement, and a little fear push me off of my game.

I need to find a good girl, a girl that will be easy and let me do things my way. Denali Street is my favorite location for watching the girls. Like a moth attracted to the fire or whatever light, I find myself back uptown here, just waiting.

A light tap on my passenger window snaps me back into the moment. I can hear a soft sexy voice murmuring for my attention, "Hey cowboy, you looking for a good time tonight? Take me for a ride I will never forget," she says.

I respond, "Well, I just may be looking for a good time, as you say. What will that ride cost me?"

"You act like a cop. Are you a cop?" she asks.

"No. Not me. I would never think of being a cop," I retort.

"I'll give you the midnight special. Two-hundred dollars gets you the full ride. What do you think is Sugar Plum worth the two-hundred dollars?" she asks.

"Sugar Plum, that just might work for me. Tonight, I need you to do things a little differently for me if you get in. I am going to call you Ingra. Will that be okay, Ingra?"

With a mischievous smirk, she replies, "Ingra is about to get naughty."

"Jump in and let's get this party s-s-started," I plead.

When she gets in her short skirt, pulled up her thighs distracts me. I see a tear in her red stocking along her inner thigh that makes me forget for a moment what we are here to do. When she reaches over to kiss me, I grab her head and slam it off of my dashboard.

Looking stunned, she starts screaming, "Are you him?" Are you the guy? Don't kill me."

Wrestling to get her left arm secured in handcuffs, I start screaming back at her, "You're a bad girl tonight, your name is Ingra, Ingra is a bad girl. Ingra needs to be punished."

Heavy breathed, and wild-eyed Ingra is nodding no, "No, don't. Stop it, you're hurting me," she is shouting.

"Shut up!" I slap her across the left cheek with my revolver. She glares over at me with blotches of red covering her face. She seems to be burning with anger.

"I hate you. I hate you," she erupts.

The muzzle of my .38 revolver touches her forehead. I push harder, causing a red dimple to appear, "Go ahead and yell one more time. I dare you," I snarl.

Sniveling, broken and defeated, she slumps into her seat. *I haven't decided whether I want to shoot her, stab her, or strangle her yet. I am keeping an open mind with this one.*

I already have a hole dug behind my bakery right along the foundation. It is so deep I need a ladder to get down into it. No one will ever think of looking for a dead body there.

Once we get into my basement, Ingra seems spellbound by all my wildlife mounts, maybe even appalled, surrounded by these symbols of death. I am explaining the bear rug I want us to make love on with her.

"This bear is not indigenous to Alaska. It is a diminutive species from another country. It was made as a wall mount. I prefer having it on the floor. You are going to lay here on this tonight," I whisper into her ear while wrapping a dog chain around her tender neck.

After I lay her down, I open a drawer and remove a beautiful dream catcher. There is a wind chime attached to it. I tie it off on the rafter above her head. Her muffled cries seeping through the mouth gag have aroused me.

Slowly undressing, I start growling like a mad dog. I watch Ingra's body tighten in response. I can't hold back any longer. I unleash a verbal tirade, "L-l-look at you. Bad Ingra. Don't kill me. Don't kill me. Where's my ride? I want a ride. You promised a ride." Look at you; you're a half-witted little fool."

Wow! that felt good. Nudity and gore ignite my lust. Ingra's body is heaving, and her mouth is frothing. My ferocity was explosive. I have to kill this girl. The things I have done to her, I mean she has to die. I decide it's the chains.

Ingra's eyes are swelling outward from their sockets, and her last breath is a hollow bubbling sound. Her fingers are bleeding from clutching at the tightly wrapped chain. It has been a good hunt, rewarded with a great kill.

CHAPTER THIRTY-TWO

ANCHORAGE CORRECTIONAL COMPLEX

As they shuffle me down the corridor of a lower maximum-security tier, forty-five red-faced hooligans are shouting obscenities and spitting at me. *Hildebrandt has messed with the wrong guy. If I can get word to Maestro, he can clear this up. When he has me released out of this zoo, I am going scorched earth. Every girl dies from now on.*

The shouting continues, "You're dead Dirks! You killed my girlfriend! Hey, you little twerp, I am going to crush your ugly skull. No one can protect you now, Dirks."

The security procession stops me in front of cell number forty-three. One of the guards shouts out, "Open cell number forty-three." Amid the creaking and clanging of the sliding door, I can hear the muffled sighs of self-satisfaction.

After they remove my restraints, a heavily built guard pushes me into the prison cell while proclaiming, "Here's your new bedroom Dirks. Sleep tight, little man."

Once I gather myself, my eyes fall on bold black letters someone wrote across the back wall. They wrote, "I Never Loved Freedom until Now," I shake my head in agreement with the sentiment.

A swishing sound across the floor causes me to look down. A prison guard threw a pouch of Bugler tobacco and rolling papers into my cell for me and proclaimed, "Enjoy Dirks." Bugler is high-quality and consistent roll-your-own cigarette tobacco. Maybe this won't be so bad in here after all.

During midday, they opened our cells and have allowed us to mingle in the corridor. A younger guy is approaching me, "Hi. They call me Crazy in here. What's your name?" he asks.

"Dirks, Damon Dirks. Glad t-t-to meet you Crazy," I reply.

He introduces me to an older man, "This is Pops. Pops rolls all of our cigarettes for us. His fee is five cigarettes per pouch," Crazy explains

"Pops, nice to meet you. I will need your services. How does this w-w-work?" I inquire.

With a twinkle in his blue eyes, Pops responds, "Nice to meet you, Damon. Every morning after chow call, we get locked down for forty-five minutes. After the lockdown, they do a headcount. If the count is correct, they open our cells for two hours of community time."

"Come into my cell tomorrow morning after chow with your tobacco. There will be a small group of guys gathered. They will be glad to meet you," Pops explains.

In the morning, after chow call, Pops is alone in his cell when I enter. He is sitting cross-legged in the middle of his bed with cardboard balanced on his knees. He has a pile of tobacco situated in the center of the cardboard, and I see about fifteen cigarettes already rolled pushed off to the side.

His smile is infectious, "Sit Dirks, have a seat over here," he motions toward the corner of his bunk. Shaking my head no, I point at the floor.

"I'll s-s-sit down here if you don't mind, Pops. I am used to sitting on the ground during my hunts," I reply. Pops head is gently nodding up and down, but his eyes are blazing holes through my head. He seems slightly disgusted. His eyes have lost their twinkle.

I am becoming frightened by my encounter with this man. The fear starts pushing everything else out of my brain. Pops starts speaking, "Damon, let me regale you with a tale if I may?"

I usually ignore a guy like this, but he has my attention and tobacco so I stay sitting on the floor listening to him as he speaks with me. "Damon, there's a rumor of a hermit living up in Arctic Valley."

"They say he has the soul of a hungry rabid wolf. He was cursed from a young age by an Indian shaman. Destined to wander from sordid kill to kill, his lust will never be satisfied."

"Rumors and speculation say he uses black magic and eats parts of his victims, sometimes cutting pieces out of their bodies while they are still alive. He then makes the women watch as he sears their flesh over the open fire and devours it in front of them."

"This is a disturbing conversation Pops," I shout. "I did not do those things you are accusing me of. I never killed anybody up in Arctic Valley. I think I want to leave now," but Pops is looking right through me.

A shuffling sound gets my attention. Out of the corner of my eye, I see three bulky shadows storming into Pops cell. A confused, sudden, and forceful attack ensues. Unexpectedly, I am fighting for my life.

When the knee connects with my stomach, I curl into a standing fetal position. One of my assailants jumps up and comes down, driving his elbow into the back of my neck. They are all screaming, "Someone's getting dead tonight. You're dead, Dirks."

I buckle to my knees. My vision is blurred. Pops is standing up on his bed in the corner, staying clear of the melee. I reach my hand up toward him, trying to speak, but no words come out.

An assailant has removed his belt and is wrapping it around my neck. I can see Pops is standing up and tying a small rope through the ceiling grate. It looks like a hangman's noose. The bombardment of verbal abuse continues to assail me.

"Dirks, you puke. Get him up over here. Tie this around his neck. Stop squirming, Dirks." They all start slapping me and spitting on me. Pops coughs a glob of thick saliva onto my face.

Someone is yelling, "Get him up over here, get him up," the struggle is violent.

Pops shouts the command, "Let him go."

A shriek bellows from deep within the beast's belly. Dirks is kicking in the air. His gurgling is a confession that death has no friends. Swirling thoughts, infectious and spiteful, consume his last moments, "You deserve this, Dirks. Tonight is your time to dance with death, Dirks."

www.ingramcontent.com/pod-product-compliance
Lightning Source LLC
Chambersburg PA
CBHW071955070426
42453CB00008BA/795

ISBN Number: 978-1-63747-027-5
eBook ISBN Number: 978-1-63747-028-2

Library of Congress Number: 2021938428

Copyright 2021 Robert Algeri
—First Edition—

Manufactured in the United States of America